The Heart of Loving

by Eugene Kennedy

Argus Communications · NILES, ILLINOIS 60648

Copyright © Argus Communications 1973

FIRST EDITION

Jacket Design and Book Illustrations by
Ron Bradford.

Printed in the United States of America.
All rights reserved. No portion of this
book may be reproduced in any form without
the written permission of the publisher.

Argus Communications
7440 Natchez Avenue
Niles, Illinois 60648

International Standard Book Number: 0-913592-19-6
Library of Congress Catalog Card Number: 73-81466

F. S.

CONTENTS

CHAPTER 1

WHERE

DOES LOVE BEGIN?

Sadly, many people know more about the way love ends than the way it begins. America seems to be a land in which love is mourned almost as much as it is celebrated. The solemn, set faces of the hurrying crowd mask a bittersweet secret: love may be full of life, but it can also die. Sometimes it dies after a long illness, sometimes unexpectedly. Love may be hard to find, and yet — perhaps the cruellest thing of all — it can be lost even though we stand guard over it.

In spite of all the songs, poems, books and soap operas that have celebrated the various facets of love, very few people know where or how it begins.

Love has never been easy to track on its passage through human history. It doesn't show up on radar, or in blood counts or on any of technology's other tracking devices. Perhaps the poets have seen better than most of us the shape of its trailing arc across our lives. Even for them, however, the task has always been difficult and has never been finished. They tell us of the longing deep in our souls for the experience of love. The sighs all around us tell us how much people want real love and how vulnerable people become in its pursuit. Perhaps people feel that if they knew better love's beginnings, they would have to face less of its ending. That is why they ask questions.

Can I trust this to be love? Anxiety about love is intense enough to make the ground tremble in our culture. It is one subject which merges the generations, bridging the heralded gaps between them in a common concern for friendship and personal relationships. Some older people recognize the yearning in the pains of their loneliness. Even at the end of life they feel undernourished by memories and still want the presence of another person — a person who shares and·cares. And the young, even after their enthusiasm for revolution and protest has waned, still hunger for an understanding of love's secrets.

They want love, the force as mysterious and powerful as the wind that binds people together in devotion to each other. They want someone close, someone to share a view of life with, someone with whom they feel safe enough to be themselves in the shelter that intimacy offers against the winters of life. Youth looks toward tomorrow with a question that comes from yesterday: *Can I learn to love and how do I do it?*

Close to the surface of all these questions is a somewhat undefined wonder about the beginnings of love.

...someone close,
someone to share a view
of life with,
someone to feel safe enough
to be yourself...

Anxiety about love is connected with the fact that mis-steps can easily be made in its pursuit. Love appears to lie at the end of a circling path for which no adequate maps have as yet been drawn. And there is a deeper side to this anxiety which makes it hang like a dead weight in the soul of man.

The very sound of this next question is almost too much to bear. *Can love last, or is it doomed to die?* Can I love another person throughout a lifetime, or must I talk myself into it, covering up the inevitable loss of love with the faint smile of a survivor in a Golden An-niversary photograph? Is it, as Tolstoy said, that love is bound to burn out as a candle is before the end of the night?

This painful uncertainty has made it almost fashion-able to protect one's investment in love, to buy on mar-gin and sell out when the stock is at the top, to take a profit from love before it inflicts a numbing and de-structive loss on us. To some people, love seems so un-predictable that they play it against itself in an awkward and self-defeating effort to keep it from exploding in their faces like a letter-bomb from a terrorist organiza-tion.

Can I expect love out of life? Sometimes the ravished heart of the ordinary person leads him or her to ask whether love is not just a matter of chance or dumb luck, whether it isn't akin to a prize in an oversold raffle in which any winner represents a thinly sliced fraction of the chance buyers.

Reassurance and encouragement do not help those people who, despite their longing, never seem to find love at all. Others constantly test themselves about love, wondering whether they will let it slip away through a misplay or whether they will pass it by without recognizing it. This only generates more anxiety, especially as they begin to identify with the legions of the lonely who join correspondence clubs, go on singles cruises, or take other trips or chances that may just lead to love.

Some people accept interpersonal compromises; they feel half a loaf of love is better than none, in order to get something of love's experience into their lives. Others lay traps for love, making up in their imagination what their romantic strategy lacks in reality. Others turn cynical, defending themselves against love by ruling it out even as a possibility. They quote to themselves the words of William Faulkner, "Perhaps they were right putting love into books . . . perhaps it could not live anywhere else."

Some of these agonizing questions are raised by those who think that love is an entity distinct from themselves, a guiding star or a good angel that some afternoon will strike them with a transforming wand. Love, however, cannot be imagined as separate from ourselves; it is rooted in ourselves, as much a part of us as breath and spirit, something that is born as we break out of our self-concern, something that grows with our responses to other persons. It grows ever outward from wanting love for ourselves to its fullest form in giving it freely away just for the sake of the other.

The focus on love as an inconstant phenomenon, a moon whose rays might just luckily strike us some day,

Love
lives always
with the
possibility
of pain
and
death.

makes it almost impossible to see that love does not happen to us. We make it happen as we open ourselves to others.

Can I be confident that I am not just loving myself, or loving the idea of love? This is a logical question for those who know that love's presence is linked with their own personality. Oversophistication in the psychological arts has become overkill for persons so locked into self-analysis that they destroy their spontaneity in the process. We can be captives of our own unconscious motivation and, in the name of loving, carry on a passionate affair with our own image and likeness. Our search for love later in life may be an external effort to bridge some early gap in our personality. It may be an attempt to make up for some loss, now gone from memory, which, like Citizen Kane's boyhood sled, *Rosebud*, remains a hidden, driving force in our lives. Some people become so introspective and suspicious of love that they give it no room to grow inside themselves.

These questions, the banners of splintered hearts everywhere, all say something true about life. They are not just the excuses of the faint-hearted nor the bitter rationalizations of those who have been hurt by love. Truth resides in each of them, and yet love remains as a deeper and more transforming possibility, like the sunlight that turns magical the stately ruins of our human condition. That is where you find love — in the incomplete yet always promising human situation we all share.

That is why love always lives with the possibility of pain and death.

17

Because of its utter realism, love retains the power to gives us joy and peace in midst of our struggles and fears. Love does not deny life; if anything, it forces us to look it more firmly in the eye. Love bids us to discover strengths we hardly suspect are in our possession. Love gives a shape to our energies so that we can finally possess the meaning of our lives. Love cannot be understood free from the treacherous snares and entanglements of human existence; it co-exists with pain and tragedy, making them bearable and integrating them into the patterns of our lives. Love can only be understood as the energy that binds the ravelled strands of ourselves together, as the power that allows us to reach across the chasms of our imperfections and to know the communion with another which defies our selfishness and our shortcomings. Love is the mystery at the heart of our own mysteries, the reality on which our lives are ultimately constructed, the flawed truth that is exactly right for man.

Lewis Mumford once wrote, "Let us confess it: the human condition is always desperate." And so it is. The human condition is a state in which everything can go wrong, where plans regularly fall apart, friends hurt each other, and the innocent person often inherits back taxes and suffering rather than the earth. Love is a response to the utter imperfection of our humanity, the fire that forges together our varied weaknesses so that our meaning as persons can emerge. One of our longstanding difficulties about love hinges on our overinvestment in perfection. This is a serious difficulty, especially for Americans who traditionally like to make things work, especially things like love, which some people say can

Love
is a response
to the utter imperfection
of humanity,
the fire
that forges together
our weaknesses
so that our
meaning as
persons can
emerge.

never work at all. One of the reasons Americans experience perennial difficulties with love is that we take it too seriously, that we look on it as a problem to be solved. Our Yankee ingenuity has always solved all problems. Another reason why we Americans suffer so much about love is that we try so hard to make it perfect, to get it right once and for all, and in the process, to disprove the poetic insight that true love follows an unsmooth course.

This urge for the perfect experience of love fits the familiar cultural myth that once man and woman have gotten themselves into the proper romantic focus they will sail into an unending sunset. They will live happily ever after with no strife or misunderstanding. Real love is actually much stronger than this vision. Human love is made for people who show signs of having lived; people who become wrinkled, get gray hair, and accumulate scars. Real love is powerful enough to accompany imperfect persons through the shifting stages of their lives together.

Love lives only in the unfinished hearts of ordinary, struggling persons. The idea of any love so sheerly perfect that there is no room in it for imperfections has no room in it for what is truly human. Many people feel uncomfortable in ultramodern settings in which smooth plastic surfaces have no seams, and the enamel sheen on walls and furniture hurts rather than rests the eyes. There is something disconcerting about those perfect model rooms where velvet ropes keep human beings from entering because they might leave marks of their humanity behind. In the massive brick wall, the eye is immediately and naturally drawn to the one brick slightly out of place—as the sure sign of a human person's hand in the construction.

Man is simply not made for the state of perfection, nor for the achievement of impossible dreams, no matter how much they may quicken his pulse or raise the fever of his idealism.

By nature man is suited for growth that is uneven, surprising, and forever challenging. This kind of growth goes along with never quite getting things right, with making mistakes and falling short, with the helpless feeling that the best moments of life slip away from us before we quite recognize them. Yet perfection haunts man still; man refuses to accept himself as he is and is ashamed rather than forgiving of his own mistakes.

Life is not kind to those who insist that there is a perfect mode of living. This tyrannical thesis kills the beginning of love, because it estranges people from their own personalities and denies them the friendship they need with themselves first, the friendship with others second. Perfectionism implies that it is not safe to appear in public until our performance is so flawless that it cannot be criticized; we cannot appear until we are so well defended that we cannot be seen. So people who demand perfection of themselves never enter very deeply into life at all. They fear that if they reveal themselves to others, their faults will easily be seen—and that others will laugh at them or ridicule them. This fear keeps them on the sidelines of life, waiting for the perfection and the safe time that never does come.

Demanding perfection can be dehumanizing and defeating. Overtraining causes athletes to go flat, just as too much rewriting destroys authors. A wildly enthusiastic and magnificently alive painting can be refined, fixed, adjusted, polished, revised, and "perfected" until it is quite dead and dull.

A fundamental truth about life, filled with implications about love, tells us that our best performances are always imperfect ones. When we try too hard to eliminate all flaws, we sacrifice our guts for bravado and our depth for a surface polish. No great work of art — and no great love — has ever appeared without the human tracings of those involved, the heroic but validating human signatures which always show through. Faultless art estranges us from the hand of the man who carved or painted it. Similarly, love that tries to take on invulnerability through perfection drains away from man and woman the vitality they need to share life in a truly human way.

Back in the caverns of history, in our folklore and myths, we read the story of man's quest for himself and for loving relationships through the trials and separations of an imperfect condition. The faulted road that leads to any human triumph tells us of the futility of trying to get everything exactly right in our lives. In stories old or new, it is where the individual stumbles and falls that he always discovers the treasure. There is always a coupling of human failure to human realization. Love does not exist on the sterile parabolas of mathematical curves, isolated from passion, misunderstanding, or the need to seek and to give forgiveness. Love incorporates us into an imperfect search for the kind of sharing through which we draw gently together the constantly fraying edges of our lives and relationships. It is the miracle that enables us to do what is right even in the face of all that is wrong in us.

But love is dangerous, too. Certainly this is one of the reasons why we are so preoccupied with creating perfect conditions for loving. There are many schools of thought about this. One school portrays love as a species of entrapment in earthly concerns that keeps us from flying free in a more spiritualized way. Another views love as an illusion tempting us into treacherous corners where the burden of love finally crushes us to death. Love is dangerous, there is no doubt about that, because we discover it only on that fine edge of existence where the balance is always delicate. Love is seeded with the danger of loss, the pain of separation, the mystery of death, the grieving that only the deeply loving can understand. That is why love is often described as a risk, a response that can only be made by detaching ourselves from safe positions in order to reach out to another person. Love is dangerous because breaking out of our own shell makes us prey to the circling vultures of cynicism and despair. Love is dangerous because it demands that we sense and accept our individuality, that we take responsibility for who we are and what we do when we draw close to another person. Love bristles with danger, because it demands that we purge ourselves of selfish inclinations to use each other rather than to find and share life with each other. Love is dangerous because it involves us in a process of continuous search into places where we have not yet traveled and where we might easily lose our way.

Love lets us get at our true selves, but it is not easy. We shed the resistant layers of narcissistic self-concern in order to discover and bring into life the full force of our personality. Love allows us to touch others and to free them for a more meaningful participation in life. Love grows only in the earth that rumbles with the energies of the human spirit, in the soil that can crack open at our feet and engulf us at any moment. Here it is that we can also harness love's energies and become more completely ourselves so that we have something to give away or share.

There is an active, intimate dimension for each of us in loving. At no moment is love separate from the stage of growth we have reached. In other words, love grows as we grow. Whether it and we flourish depends on our affirming and accepting the consequences of becoming more of ourselves in each moment. That is the nature of slow but sure growth. Love is not a soft or shapeless commodity; it has hard edges that realistically frame our view of ourselves and others. Love is not just sentimental comfort in the midst of the wreckage of life; rather it is the motivational spark for carrying on, for reaching out even when we are wearied of reaching out. Love makes this easier because it allows us to see someone reaching toward us at the same time.

Love lights up the shadowed pathways of life so that we can recognize each other. The truth about ourselves is revealed in that open space of intimacy where the tenderness of our lover is our only safeguard from being hurt. Love is not a finished product; it is an always-developing enterprise, urging us to discover more about our own possibilities and enabling us to bring these to light in others as well. You cannot, however, enter the mysteries of loving with your guard up. And there is no way you can take love by force. Love comes easily to those who still believe even though they have been disappointed, to those who still hope even though they have been betrayed, to those who try to love even though they have been hurt before.

Love is for the average person, for everyone who knows that finding life's center of gravity depends on reaching each other genuinely — if imperfectly — with something that is true about ourselves.

Frequently people overlook the essentially mysterious nature of this imperfect search for love. Proust once described love as time and space measured by the heart. Love permits us to see our world in a fresh manner and to appreciate the spiritual edging of every activity man chooses in its pursuit. For example, love asks us to find ourselves at the price of yielding up false notions and selfish considerations about our personality. Love tells us that human life lies in the fulfillment of what is true and imperfect about ourselves. Some people think that talk of self-fulfillment is a kind of weakness. Fulfillment strikes its critics as an easy path, an indulgent, selfish,

At no
moment
is love
separate
from the stage
of growth
we have
reached.

and not very difficult journey. They say it is far better to take the path of self-transcendence, that stony rise that takes us up single file away from the boiling city of man below. This is frequently expressed as a notion that isolates men from each other so that they may pursue some transcendent ideal more effectively. Such a notion has made it difficult for many people to appreciate the profoundly spiritual nature of authentic love.

Nobody who has ever loved another person describes it as an easy or painless way toward fulfilling himself. Fulfillment takes place, that is true; but only through involvement and decisions which demand a surrender of part of the self — only the human heart made vulnerable experiences and enjoys the riches of the mystery. Being human is not to be feared as though it were sinful; it is where we work at healing each other. It is easier by far to escape the burden of love, to look to the mountain top where you never have to look straight into the faces of other persons. We transcend and fulfill ourselves quite directly and in ordinary ways.

Love leads to stability in our relationships, to a solid base on which to stand close to another through the years, even though we are unaware of the storms that may break on us in the future. Love is not an intermittent visitor to life. It only seems that way to people who are edgy about committing themselves to it, who allow their fear of its consequences to make them write impossible conditions into their experience of it. Love is intermittent only for the timid and isolated — those like the contemporary pseudo-romantics — who mourn love

*Love
lights up
the shadowed
pathways of life
so that we can
recognize
each other.*

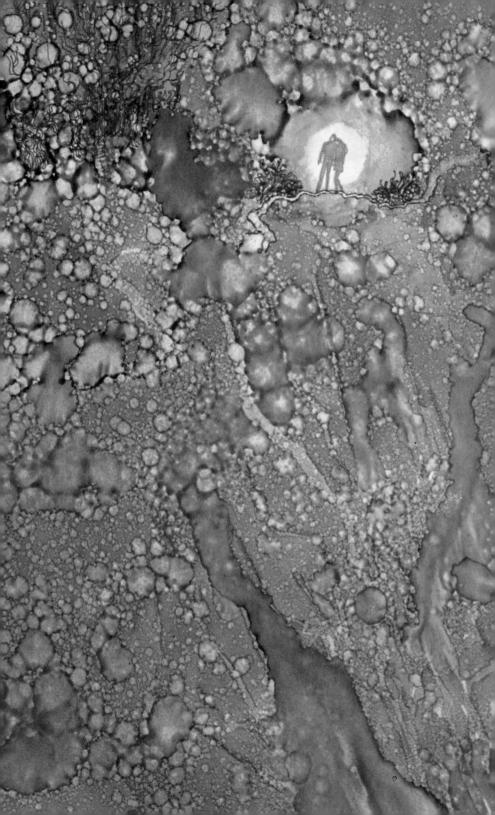

and its few moments in life, all of which have now vanished. Love was here, they say, but it's gone now. The listeners to these sentiments deserve to hear something better — something about the enduring possibilities of love.

Love deals with wholeness, directing us to a more complete picture of life as well as of ourselves. Love is an integrating impulse through which we put ourselves together and bring more of ourselves into being. That is precisely how it is creative, because it brings our total personality to life. Real love is not concerned only with parts of our relationships — such as the sexual. Love draws our attention to what we can learn only when we stand undefended before someone else. Only here do we sense the mystery of openness and sharing, not as a long-dead phenomenon, but as an active, experienced presence enabling us to know and be known by others; the light to see more deeply comes from the flame ignited by the mystery of sharing. Through love we appreciate the concrete meaning of community through the sharing of people who trust each other even though they are well aware of each other's weaknesses. Love enables us to experience healing, not as a theory or an abstract notion, but as the task we perform for each other in the midst of life that is often top-heavy with the injuries that only the intimate can inflict on each other. Love makes us mentally and emotionally conscious of who we are and what we do with each other in the course of life. Love sensitizes us to the consequences of our actions, to the special knowledge that nothing can ever be described as merely casual between people who trust each other very deeply. All things, even the smallest of them, count between true lovers. Love opens us to the depth of life in which lovers have learned to forgive themselves and each other for being human.

Love gives us a richer view of the world around us, a finer delineation of our relationships and our responsibilities for them. It breaks the bonds of a more restricted vision, of the narrowed perception that results from the defenses that close us in. A person never sees very much when he squints his eyes to shield himself or herself from whatever might happen. Love alone opens our eyes fully to everything that is beautiful and terrible in the human condition.

Love is a mystery only for those people who cannot grasp how marvelously it fits the human condition. It is easily understood by persons who recognize that it is not for sale and that it does not exist separate from us, like a bank deposit or a rainbow.

Where does love begin? It begins in an imperfect person who recognizes his imperfection and accepts it as permanent and yet ever-changing. Love begins in a human being willing to risk ridicule and hurt — to accept the danger of loss and the grief of separation in order to reach out to another person. It is in risking much that we can gain all, in giving much that we can expect to discover love.

Love is not jealous of its secrets, but it can be approached in only one way: along the broad road where we walk at least two by two, stumbling and getting in each other's way and at the same time discovering that we are each other's strength and joy.

34

Chapter 2

"LET'S TAKE THE SHORTCUT."

"DO WE HAVE ENOUGH TIME?"

There is always some restyled and subtle brand of perfectionism on the cultural market. It is not at all surprising to see man returning to older dreams through the current nostalgia craze. We presume that a simpler and more spacious age existed, perhaps in the generation just before this one, an age when we may have had less but seemed to enjoy life more. The latest proof of this, of course, is the romanticizing of America's depression which currently flickers across television and movie screens. These programs echo a time lost, something we might get again if only we could strip ourselves of the burdens we have acquired since that time. "The Good

Old Days" weren't always good, but they always seem to be remembered that way. Men would like to transport themselves back to an era in which they seemed to be in close touch with their values and ideals. This search illustrates the human heart's perennial vulnerability to half-formed visions and to the promissory notes of the imagination. Man seems willing to believe and to try whatever tells him that, despite the proverb, he *can* go home again, that there are short-cuts back to innocence. Men want to believe in the time machines, elixirs, and other ways of getting free of their accumulated life histories. All they need is to shatter the chains of their repression and slip onto the newest high road of discovery and self-fulfillment.

There are different faces to these movements, but they hang together around a common theme: one must break through the flow of life and escape the devouring engines of progress. Sensitivity sessions, transcendental meditation, far eastern religion, horoscopes or expanded awareness through the chemistry of drugs all offer similar Utopian promises. The attraction seems to be something like, "If the *movement* will do it, then *I* won't have to do it." No one should question the sincerity of people who look to these movements for an answer to the stifling experiences of their lives. Man's search for his wholeness must be viewed through compassionate eyes which probe deeply to understand rather than to judge. Nevertheless, the recurring themes of contemporary perfectionists must be reviewed because they present an unrealistic and deceptive program to men and women who want to understand the secrets of friendship and love. No one can reach the goal of adult relationships effortlessly or magically; there is no skipping any of the steps that lead to having a friend and sharing a love.

Freedom from constraint is the dominant motif in the latest music of perfection — no bonds, no entangling alliances, no debts, no obligations. This philosophy says that anything which represses human beings tends to disfigure them and make the realization of their own identity much more difficult. Any limitation represents an infringement on a person's potential which would otherwise successfully be realized. "Why spoil our relationship with marriage?" is one way this logic runs; it can be reduced to the assertion that people will spring to their fullness in a world cleansed of demands or claims, in an environment where freedom means being able to put one's own impulses first. Some people, sincerely, though perhaps, naively, believe that this is what it means to trust another person — to allow him or her to do whatever he or she cares to do without restraint or interference, without establishment of even common sense limits.

This version of the perfection of the natural man is not simply a revolt against Victorianism and its stringent and suffocating repression of free choice. It possesses a self-conscious kind of righteousness. Freedom from constraint will liberate man from the neurosis which prevents him from leading a totally natural life. This leads to strange and selfish versions of love that are ultimately as destructive as they are disappointing. This freedom is not informed with a basic sense of what actually goes on in personal relationships. It overlooks, in a tragedy repeated beyond telling, the limits within which love is experienced between human beings. It fails to acknowledge the essentially imperfect nature of human relationships that requires us always to surrender something of ourselves in the heart of genuine love. The spacious freedom that allows a person to withdraw from the adult world into the fantasy of an infantile environment is actually regressive. In a childish world the individual is sheltered and cared for even though he may not be conscious of it. The shelter and care given by others allow the child the freedom to be narcissistic and self-centered in the early stages of life. Part of the process we call growing up is the recognition that something other than self is at the center of the universe. When an adult tries to recapture this same child-like freedom, he actually makes himself ineligible for the experience of mature love. Second childhoods never duplicate the originals.

This exaltation of self-reliant emotional experience as an end in itself is another prime tenet in the latest book of perfectionism. It underscores self-satisfying experience as self-justifying by removing it from the context of life and the complex of relationships in which we all live. When these are stripped away, the individual need not pay attention to the past nor to the future; he can focus on the present in which he can expand his consciousness in a variety of ways. A shift in this direction is suggested by the studies which reveal that expressive goals rather than traditional ones are more appealing to some young people now. They prefer those activities

40

which provide them with an immediate sense of participation and emotional reward rather than those activities which are carried out with a view to some more distant goal, because this defers gratification and requires some constraint on impulses. In other words, they do not want to wait. Deferred gratification is equated with nongratification. This can account for some of the great popularity of Polaroid pictures, for example, and for phrases like, "He's a *now* person." The expansion of present consciousness is practically a business in American culture. The "now" trend taps into people's longing for friendship and love and promises them these rewards as painlessly as possible. People want love. If there is an easier way to get it, they will try for it.

Contemporary perfectionists might not identify themselves as such, yet they all offer products which imitate the outcomes normally associated with the slower and sometimes agonizing experiences of ordinary life. In no area is this more clear than in the explosion of pseudo-creativity which has littered the sections of many cities with arts and crafts whose crudity reflects the lack of discipline that went into their making. Everything looks better, according to the pamphleteers of a world conquered by drugs, when the acid is working and the person is absorbed in the immediate experience which drugs provide. That is why there is so much emphasis on "getting a high," on penetrating the moment without any perspective of its overall relationship to life. Drugs, alcohol, "liberated" sex, and other favorites of the counter-culture promise the new, mystical feeling without any echoes of that old-time religion.

The problem is that there are no short-cuts to the experience of love; there are cruel and expensive delusions, but no love. Persons who would have the reward of love without the vulnerability that is always an intimate part of it will be forever disappointed — or hoodwinked.

Instead of some moderate realism about the coexistence of sacrifice and joy in life, the new emphasis on immediate experience attempts to kill off two dimensions of reality which are closely related to learning how to love. The death of time is involved in the celebration of immediate experience. Time, according to Norman O. Brown, is in itself neurotic. Time is a limitation which cannot be borne by men who seize the moment, whether it is by way of a drug trip or through a far eastern, meditative self-transformation in a rock garden which, because it has no plants to change with the seasons, floats in a timeless pebbled sea. The result is always the same: the perfection of the self is dependent on the freeze frame of peak experiences. Time is an enemy of the newly liberated who feel that technology has made clocks into ravening goddesses which have feasted on men's souls. When a person can get away from time, there is no need to worry about what one has done, nor what the consequences of one's present behavior will be. *Now* becomes everything.

Closely allied to the death of time is the death of care. The escape from involvement with another individ-

No one
can reach the goal
of adult relationships
effortlessly or magically.
There is
no skipping any
of the steps that
lead to having
a friend and
sharing a
love.

ual is implicit in the character of much of this contemporary effort at self-fulfillment. If you can stand outside of time and outside of the one-to-one relationships which demand a unique and individual response, then you are freed from two of the most severe limitations in the human condition. One can seem to recapture what appears to be a lost and guiltless innocence through this maneuver, presumably making a beachhead on an earlier and carefree time in life.

Care is a profound word, however. When its meaning is eclipsed or glossed-over by an immature effort to make life into a playground, our sense of humanity is violated and diminished.

It is not surprising that the culture which has given birth to these kinds of movements has footnoted them with events that describe their true nature very well. It is no accident, for example, that the individuals who advocate no-fault sexual promiscuity have been observed to intersperse their activities with strange journeys back to childhood, to a renewed interest in Winnie the Pooh, comic books, and the Mousketeers. Childhood was a time when one was cared for, a precious time before the dawn of responsibility for caring for others. Life went on without any of the disturbing problems that come with really caring actively for others. It is not surprising, then, to note the muting of the contrast between the sexes that has become commonplace in recent years. Although it is easy to read too much into this, still it could be symbolic of a childhood time of life when the differences between male and female could not be perceived and so did not provide the dilemmas of an adult relationship.

In the same manner, much of the activity of some young people in communes and in shared quarters in college dormitories resembles children playing house rather than adults living in a grown up and demanding relationship with each other. In some of these situations, there is surprisingly little sex despite the closeness of the living. Many of the participants, particularly the men, are not looking for lovers, but for new versions of the mother who always cleaned up after them — the mother who let them go on being cared for but crippled them in the process; they cannot comprehend any other kind of relationship.

It is obvious that not all young people are involved in efforts at self-development that end up being self-deceptive. It is, however, worth reflecting on these central themes for two reasons. First, those who eagerly respond to the visions of self-fulfillment are frequently individuals whose own character structure makes them particularly vulnerable in these situations. Secondly, those healthy persons who are still seeking for the values of deep and enduring love need to be reassured about their own instincts in this regard. The latter frequently feel alienated or wonder if they are out of step and out of style; they need to be supported in their search for deeper values. True fulfillment has never come in an instant, nor through chemistry, nor from breaking away from constraints in an effort to penetrate the *now* of experience. There is simply no pursuit of life which safely frees us from a healthy sense of our own limitations or the inevitable boundaries of personality that we must acknowledge if we are truly to love and be loved by other persons.

The free man understands the hard edges of existence. He does not deceive himself into thinking that an escape from constraint will automatically place him on the high road to individual perfection. Freedom is conditioned by reality, by a sense of being linked to other persons who have rights and lives separate from our own. Love comes to life for the individual who has a deep sense of his own identity. This means that he is aware of being a distinct person, a unique presence in life, who can see and respond to others as separate and unique in their own right. Only when a person sees this clearly does he begin to understand the meaning of care as concern for someone other than himself. What must die is precisely the self-absorption which goes along with narcissistic self-concern. When we see only ourselves, we make it impossible to see others, and we make the beginnings of love impossible.

You do not show trust to a person by letting him do anything he feels like; neither do you demonstrate much trust by deceiving him about the nature of the world nor by promising rewards he can achieve only by hard work. The road to love demands that we constantly improve our awareness of others, that we progressively peel away the layers of self-concern that isolate us and make us exiles from love. A free sense of ourselves is always related to a respectful sense of others so that we move with integrity in their lives, aware of their needs as well as our own, and do not trample on them because we think that our own claims are more important. It is clear that too much concentration on the immediate moment, with the consequent effort to kill both time and care, also dehumanizes us and makes the possibility of true friendship and personal fulfillment more remote than ever. Only the individual who locates himself fairly accurately in space and time with other persons — facing up to the limitations which these impose on his freedom in life — ever senses the continuity and meaning of his own existence. Only as he develops a sense of time can he develop the patience to work through some of the essential experiences of loving and being loved by another person.

There is no way to escape the demands of time. Lovers who hurt each other may wish that they could heal the wounds in an instant. It would be nice if it worked that way, but everybody knows that it never does; time has its way with us, and we must *live* through the long moments of healing. Only genuine love gives people the strength to pass through this time successfully together. This is beyond understanding for those who concentrate only on the moment and who flee from time as from an enemy.

Only lovers can grow old together without fear or discouragement. Lovers who enter into time also conquer it: that is one of the paradoxes of love. Lovers come to understand, that, within the limits of time, they appreciate the timeless quality at the heart of their own relationship with each other. Enter into time and you transcend it; try to escape it and you cannot — and you miss love in the bargain. Lovers do not have to kill time; they have learned something of its meaning, and they stand together no longer afraid of it.

In the same way, friends know that they cannot lead a carefree life — that there is something illusory in the kind of "play" that is advocated in *Playboy*. Genuine playfulness is a byproduct of successful intimacy; only persons who truly care for each other can know the rich and truly recreative meaning of playfulness. The person who eliminates a sense of care from life (who, for example, no longer worries about the consequences of a seduction) has cut himself off from ever understanding the meaning of mature love. The playfulness of adults is very different from the mock innocence of those people who cluster together in an effort to reclaim a childhood time when the sexes were alike and life was largely make-believe. Adult lovers have separated themselves from the stage of being cared for — and a thousand deaths go into giving this up — and they are now able to put their strength into caring for others. To do this effectively they must marshall their own energies and tap into their own healthy aggressions. They cannot just stand around waiting for life to wash over them with refreshing and nourishing tides.

Adult lovers know that they are really not neutral and that it is not sameness that brings them happiness, but a healthy sense of the differences between themselves and others that make life meaningful. They are not unacquainted with their own identity or deeply afraid of placing their flawed true selves into close relationship with another person. It is impossible for individuals who lack a sense of their own identity to share anything with others. They may merge, like characterless protoplasm, but without a sense of themselves, they are locked out of the excitement and the magic of the contrasting relationship that is the most different of all — that between man and woman.

It should not surprise us to find some men complaining of sexual impotence as a contemporary problem. It may be a sign of powerlessness, of strengths unmarshalled, of a sense of the self that has never come together successfully. Rollo May, in his book, *Power and Innocence*, eloquently describes the lack of a capacity for loving found in the individual who has not successfully integrated the aggressive components of his personality. He suggests that such powerless persons are the products of structureless situations which try to create a land of no limits and a focus on the immediate moment cut off from both past history and future consequences. "These structureless families which operate supposedly on love without power lead to the development of rootless children, who later in life rebuke their parents for having never said no to them." They are persons cared for so much by others that they now lack the capacity to care for themselves adequately. These individuals cannot evoke the strengths which they need in order to survive and to discover and express love in their own lives. They are too accustomed to having things done for them, to living in the sheltered universe of extended childhood from which they should have separated themselves long ago. The sad part for these people is that they seek love

*Love
comes to life
for the
individual
who has a deep
sense of
his own
identity.*

through the foreshortened experiences that turn them in on themselves and make love even more difficult to understand or achieve.

Pseudo-trust and pseudo-love are not strong enough to sustain people through the dimension of time which they cannot escape. The lessons of caring are doubly hard for those who have not learned much about giving it to others. Their impotence is an inheritance from parents who, in the name of love, deprived them of power and of learning to exercise their own power over themselves. Their rebellions, as May suggests, are often unrelated to the actual events which they claim as their motives. They are rather symbolic assaults on a world which they hope will respond by giving some structure to their lives. It is their very impotence which causes them to strike out, their failure to possess a sense of themselves as defined in space and time that fills them with longing and uncertainty about their lives. This is as much a motivation for their experimentation with sex as anything else. It is why they are tempted by a mindless slogan on the poster that says if you meet another person and you somehow strike it off for an instant then that is beautiful. Subsequently, you must pass on, cutting the incident off as though it had no roots and no possible effects on the future.

"This endeavor to love with the renunciation of power," says Rollo May, "is a product of the tendency toward pseudoinnocence. It underestimates the difficulty of loving. . . ." That is the major problem of the moment: people cannot find love through easy means; that only makes them long more desperately for it.

53

*Lovers
who enter
into time also
conquer it.*

The pain and confusion surrounding friendship and love are not new to our generation. Men and women have always had to find their own way to the heart of love, and they have always had to face the suffering that is both the prelude and accompaniment to a joyful and meaningful life. However, the present two-fold refusal to deal realistically with the human condition has contributed to the impotence and estrangement of a whole generation of Americans. This new surge toward paradise outside of time makes authentic love more remote and the experience of deep passion more difficult.

Love is found by those who can live with some degree of comfort with human nature as it is. This does not mean a sense of defeat in the face of the fates that finally conquer. Love is only active when we have a vision of man that neither rejects him as bad nor attempts to restore him to a primitive and deceptive innocence. Neither image of man permits us to discover or respond to the meaning of love, that mysterious power that touches us only when we are real. Love has never come to the perfectionists who do not understand human nature. Love is the prize for those who recognize, accept, and try to deal constructively with the varied strengths and weaknesses in the human condition. Becoming a person has nothing to do with perfection, sensual or spiritual. It depends on affirming ourselves with a consciousness of the shifting and often contrary aspects of our personalities. It comes from the gentle honesty that does not blink at savage depths; it comes out of the wisdom that is not surprised by man's blend of integrity and wickedness. Man loves in order to put all this together under the category of his own identity, to husband his strengths and discipline his reckless urges, to forge a personality that can be shared with others. Man is called patiently and forgivingly to go as deeply as possible.

This opens a couple to authentic mystical experiences, because it incorporates them in the living mystery of love in the human condition. Man and woman achieve a relative balance as they love together through life. Their perilous life is made secure by the love which, like sunlight on the scattered glass of a rose window, fuses its discordant elements into something beautiful and unique.

To love is the only condition of this exhausting and enlivening voyage; that is what makes it bearable and glorious. The utter vulnerability that characterizes the passage together is an absolute essential. Love and vulnerability are inseparable in the journey that involves lovers in time and care and frees them from fearing them.

*Love
is found
by those who can
live with some
degree of comfort
with human nature
as it is.*

Chapter 3

THE HARD PART

Falling in love seems as easy as it is attractive in those early moments when it is all glowing magic but not yet fire.

The hard part is staying in love: there is the challenge. It begins right after the first, long, lighter than air, free-floating fall that seems like an experience that will last forever.

There are too many stunned and hurt people around who have been engaged and disengaged, married and unmarried, loved and unloved, for us not to question this idea. But most of us believe that we are the exceptional case, *Love Story* without the leukemia, a tale of devotion as yet untold in a cynical world.

Falling in love sometimes seems like the untroubled moments in the rerun of the newsreel of some disaster. For example, as we watch the handsome young president and his wife smiling and waving to the Dallas crowd, a terrible feeling rises in us: a naive but disturbed sense that we might still avert the tragedy, if. If. That *if* underscores the hard part of staying in love. If we can avoid the tragedies that kill it, the tragedies whose signals are always present but usually unnoticed, we can stay in love. The death scene of love is often played by the broken-hearted in their imaginations. They try to tease out the meanings they did not grasp when everything seemed full of sunlight. *If* is a bad scar on the souls of the persons who have fallen out of love.

The death or serious illness of too many marriages around us tells us that lovers cannot make it if they fly blind. A shattering crash awaits those who believe that lovers can fall, weightlessly entwined, forever. Nobody would — or would want to — eliminate the crests of feeling that go with romance. That would be like trying to hose down the flames leaping from the sun. Both are signs of the energies involved; but, like everything else in life, they must be viewed in proper perspective if they are to be understood at all. Something in real love searches for balance, for a way of tempering the strength of involvement with a sense of realism. Love does not begin until a man and a woman fall out of balance through responding to each other; its continuation, however, depends on their discovering and maintaining a new balance that is right for them.

Staying in love depends on a healthy recognition and integration of all the energies — positive and negative, mature and immature — that make up the personalities of the individuals concerned. Anything else involves people in trying to love in an atmosphere that is so cleansed of the jumbled burdens of humanness that they no longer recognize either themselves or each other. Love, like fragile Camille, coughs and dies in such rarified air; it only flourishes in that blend of strong and weak elements where we all really live.

The notion of the balance involved in love is not novel. It does not surprise anyone who has heard the amateur psychologists, some of them quite unaware of what they are saying, tell us that love is very close to hate. However, experienced lovers realize that the opposite of love is not hate — the opposite of love is apathy. You must feel strongly to love, there is no doubt of that. The lover incorporates all of himself — his aggression along with his tenderness — in reaching out to his beloved. If he leaves one part of himself out, he destroys the balance and strikes a death blow to love. That, unfortunately, is why so much love is only remembered, as if it occurred in a different world to which the person can no longer return.

Love gets lost for those who do not or will not understand that it only takes root in the soil of the human situation. Anything that grows there demands attention all of the time as well as determined pruning at least part of the time. Love wants to grow, but this healthy impulse is conditioned by and filtered through our human responses at every step of its development. Balance is, therefore, necessary — a delicate equilibrium that maintains the right values in stability throughout a lifetime. Keeping a balance may be something like the task of the aerialist: balancing is precarious, but it is also the strength which the performer relies on in order to achieve his goals. The lover has one added hazard, however: there is no net to catch him if he loses balance and falls. Love grows stronger in the tension that builds up as a man and woman strive to find a balanced relationship. There is always the danger of a long fall, because the best things in life — in a mystery almost beyond explaining — arise in those situations where everything can go right and yet, with just a slight shift, may go completely wrong instead.

That is what makes love such a vital and fascinating phenomenon, even when we behold it in others. Love involves a balance keen enough to make us shiver, and yet reliable enough to generate a sweet and calming peace and strength. That is why the meeting of man and woman is perennially intriguing, and, as embodied in individual men and women, why it has endured as one of the great themes of all history. Long-dead lovers retain the power to move us profoundly; we still feel the vibrations they sent while working into and remaining in relationship with each other. This mystery is too profound to evaporate with their passing; something of this constructive tension hangs in the air over the tombs of lovers and in any place where they are remembered. It is a sign, of course, that true lovers never die, that the strength of their relationship is something we can feel even when they are not in our midst.

Lovers — whether Abelard and Eloise or Tracy and Hepburn — capture our imagination and our respect because they give off the sparks of life that still light the way for us. Mankind never tires of the stories of true lovers, not because they are rare or because they are often tinged with tragedy, but because they overflow with life. Even when we do not recognize this, we somehow sense it and respond to it.

Balance is not some shrewd, interpersonal trick, a clever mutual manipulation which gives the appearances of a relationship without any of its substance. No one can play-act his way into the risks and sharing of those who keep working at their love for each other. To keep responding against a tide of difficulties, changes, and saddening surprises is the measure of true love. It is only as rare as the individuals who are willing to say "Yes" to all, rather than just a part, of what it asks.

It is in the act of responding to each other that the self of each person is tested; it is through that continuing honest effort that we become intensely aware of our faults and yet somehow rise above them. Were it not for this constant challenge to reach out to each other, a reality at the core of real love, it is unlikely that lovers would strike any kind of living balance at all. It is this sense of realism — the ability to face each other's assets and liabilities without blinking — that allows us to heal each other through love. Only the lovers who see quite clearly are able to make the journey of life together. Love is not blind, no matter what you may have heard to that effect. Everything about lovers, good and bad, is involved in their life together, and they have no need to deceive themselves or each other about their identities.

This is the simple, human reason that we have love at all: we would never know who we are without it.

Problems are bound to arise for persons who lack a sense of realism about themselves; these individuals either will not face or prefer to misinterpret the facts of life about themselves and each other. Love is also beyond those who eliminate risk from their lives by committing their identity in a very guarded way to the possibilities of a relationship. This cautious behavior is characteristic of persons so tormented by the fear of failure that they play life and love too much like a game. They resemble the nonachievers described in psychological research who either select a goal that is so easy they cannot possibly fail or choose one that is so beyond them they cannot possibly succeed. In either case, they are freed of the responsibility of trying, and so they are freed of risk, and no one can hold their failure against them.

Love cannot be played in this manner. Risk is beautiful. Indeed, half of the unhappiness in the world would be lifted away if we could create the conditions in which persons would feel safe enough to take a chance to be more truthful with each other.

The achiever—in life and in love—chooses goals which match the tensely balanced possibilities of failure and success; he must extend himself in order to achieve his goal, but he only does this out toward the edge of his capabilities, where he may fail as well.

People sometimes fall in love with the idea of falling in love. This makes it doubly difficult for them to see

Love
gets lost
for those who do not
or will not
understand that
it only takes root
in the soil of
the human
situation.

themselves clearly or to perceive another person as separate and distinct from them. These are the captives of dreams, of the fantasies that cause them to view others as a product of their own unadmitted needs. Such relationships constitute a modern form of idolatry, but their papier-mache substance quickly becomes apparent in the bright light of reality. "I never knew you were like that," is a tag line for loves that never really began, that remained grounded in the selves of the man and woman who had never been able to distinguish themselves from the world around them.

People who stay in love manage to do so by committing themselves to the struggle to see themselves honestly and to hide as little as possible of what they experience together in life. They have a fairly good idea of what is taking place inside themselves and they can admit and accept themselves, as the mass of contrasts which they truly are. They do not merely wallow in their own weakness or surrender to the blind force of impulse; rather, they continue to work at putting themselves together, at melding their weaknesses with their strengths so that the strengths predominate in their personalities. They can be themselves, not so harshly rigid and repressive of their feelings that they never get to know or express them, but with a slightly looser rein on them because they are confident in their capacity to control their lives. Love is an ongoing challenge, but the frightened slip back without sensing either their powers or their flaws. The average healthy individual, however, is quite capable of becoming friendly toward what he really is. And he does this — with a sense of forgiveness for his faults — as he knows and becomes known very deeply by others.

The high divorce rate in teen marriages may be associated with the fact that some young men and women are not as yet in full or comfortable possession of their personalities. They neither have a well developed feeling for themselves, nor have they gone very deeply in assaying their potential. They think the fall — as in "falling in love" — will last a lifetime. It is not long before their weak points start showing through, because these so-called weak points are actually the rough or unformed edges of themselves. This is very confusing, because the hopeful lovers suddenly seem so different, so changed from what they were when the days were filled with sunlight and good feeling. These couples do not split up; they were never intially close enough to the reality of each other for that. That is why some people survive the wreckage of an early marriage and manage to acquire a wisdom about their own identity from the harsh experience. They can then enter new relationships, in which they are frequently more successful, because they know so much more about themselves as a result of their earlier pain.

What then are some practical ways in which individuals who want love to enter and remain in their lives can prepare themselves for it? How does one deepen his active participation in his own personal integration, bringing more of himself to life in a clearer and more sharply defined sense of identity? Love begins when we take the time to become more finely attuned to our own experi-

*To
keep responding
against a tide of
difficulties, changes,
and saddening surprises
is the measure
of true love.*

ence. This does not require far eastern mysticism or adopting a hermit's lifestyle; it is a wisdom at once simpler and more readily available than that. It only requires that we pay attention to ourselves, that we start to realize that the things we say and feel contain a message for us, one that we must read carefully if we are going to possess our identity. The individual need not punish himself for his shortcomings, as he might if he thought his duty were to check up on everything he does wrong. Instead, he can listen to himself as he would to a friend who needs compassionate understanding. In fact, the process of firming up our hold on ourselves may stand or fall on whether we can give the kind of sensitive attention and forgiveness to ourselves that we sometimes lavish on others. This is a good starting point for the individual who wants to know himself or herself better.

Why might you be reluctant to listen to your deeper self? Some people stifle all sounds that come from within, preferring to live on the surface of life even when they feel the vague pain — the longing for something more — that comes from the emptiness inside them. They do not want to look at, and indeed, they prefer to hurry through life, swinging from fad to fad so they don't have to notice the subtle, cancerous spread of their own loneliness. The fundamental question for these loners is just why are they so afraid of finding out what is going on inside them. A basic understanding of their own processes of emotional reaction would give these people surprising relief and comfort. It might take months or years to sort out the various causes and as-

pects of their psychological discomfort, but such ultimate analyses are not necessary for living and loving. A
person does better if he achieves even a moderate
amount of insight; the moment an individual can accept
and forgive himself—even a little—is the moment in
which he becomes to some degree loveable. Love, after
all, is a force which need not be fullblown in order to
change a man's attitude and his whole view of life.

The instant in which we love ourselves enough to
make peace with our own imperfection we also become
loveable in the eyes of others.

It's automatic. When we see ourselves in a more understanding perspective, we open a wedge in our defenses through which others can see us more clearly and
more compassionately. It sounds simple enough; the
trouble is, people believe they must solve their problems
completely before they can get on effectively and more
lovingly in life. This is an inverse form of the perfectionism that crimped their psyches in the first place. In
love, all you need is an imperfect beginning, a limp, not
an olympic stride. Unlock the door of the self, and
others will gradually open it more fully and the trans-
formation can continue. That is precisely what is going
on in the world all around us at almost every moment.
Average and unglamorous people, weighed down with
all their liabilities, turn beautiful in each other's eyes as
they open even a little bit of themselves to each other.

Love belongs not to the superman, but to the average
man. Love lives where ordinary people can see each other

The simple,
human reason that we have
love at all is that we
would never know
who we are
without it.

plainly and unaffectedly in the human condition. Love says it is always safe to go public with the truth of ourselves.

Many people do not realize how boxed in they can become when they fail to come to terms with themselves — and how inaccessible this makes them to others. A gentle look at the manner in which we now relate to others is a good way to begin a self-examination. The way we present ourselves to others reflects quite accurately the way we look at ourselves. Thus, the man who does not trust others will probably discover that he does not trust himself much either; the person who is always in a contest with others, trying to overwhelm them even in little things, may find he is inwardly pitted against himself and is never satisfied with anything he does. The person who is always trying to save others or keep them from harm may be shielding his own personality to such an extent that nobody ever gets a good look at it.

The list of possibilities is endless, and each of us must look at his own activities with patience and a willingness to accept what is found. Self-knowledge is the ultimate prize; increased self-knowledge frees us from the prison of our own personality and makes us available for more meaningful relationships with others. It makes us, flawed though we are, eligible for falling in love.

Self-knowledge can come in many other ways, as, for example, when we observe the way we handle conflict when it arises in our lives. Our response to conflict gives us excellent clues to our own psychological definition. In conflict, a person may discover he is concerned only with his own feelings, with making sure these are taken care of before anything else. If we find we always see ourselves at center stage in every incident, then we may have another clue to our self-preoccupation. No one finds love until he or she breaks out of this trap. The closed-in self is an escape-proof prison, an airless and seamless room in which we live alone, because we cannot bear to have anyone else move in on us.

The person who wants to find love in life begins by learning with some reasonable accuracy what he is like, how far he has grown, and how willing he is to risk hurt in order to grow more fully.

That is the hard part, but it doesn't have to be the harsh part. The person who can take a struggling step toward letting more of himself out in life will find he has traveled a surprisingly long way into the deep and rich country of human love.

*Love begins
when we take
the time to become
more finely attuned
to our own
experience.*

Chapter 4

YOU'LL KNOW IT
RIGHT AWAY

The human condition has many names. Many literary references can be found that identify our human terrain as "the land of the living," the place where people are truly aware of and in contact with each other. The human condition is also called "the real world" and "firm ground" on which a realistic individual securely plants his two feet. This world is the only country in which he can love; it is the only place in which his passport to this simplest and richest of relationships is valid. If it is a landscape less than perfect, it is also the place where he can feel at home with himself and with others.

In this territory we understand that life is made up of things that are at once mysterious and yet apparently quite ordinary. What is genuinely transcendent, however, never opens itself to people who seek it in outlandish or bizarre ways. The mystical part is found in the common life of each individual who senses the human condition as the truly sacred ground of life. The path to mystery is straightforward and utterly human. That does not make it an easy road, of course, and realizing this can make us suspicious of mystery supposedly produced by exotic or manipulative methods. The highlands of the human spirit are scaled by those who embrace what is genuinely simple. This includes all the best things in our lives. Mystery is made complicated by those who do not understand it. Fake mystery doesn't get you to the inside of life. That isn't the way it happens; rather, you start at the inside and find that you are surrounded by wonder.

It is not hard to recognize the experiences from the inside of life; they reveal themselves to us in a way that is quite unaffected and yet quite demanding. You can neither be a neutral bystander, a mere admirer of these experiences, nor can you be a raconteur of them in discussion groups. As swimming can be understood only if you get in the water, so loving comes across to us only in relationship to other persons. Only in shared experience can you tap into the meaning of love, drawing on love's strength and sensing its depth at the same time. Through these experiences we make our passage into "the land of the living." We cannot enter there alone or in single file. We make our journey only as individuals who are not individualistic, persons whose inner selves are not boarded up and fenced off from the environment of life. Our experiences together enable us to recognize who we are and to appreciate the significance of life together. Without them we can only wander, lost as sailors without their guiding stars. We are left to read

The mystical
part is found in
the common life
of each individual
who senses the
human condition as
the truly sacred
ground of life.

"How To" books and imagine that life is very complicated after all.

The experiences of substance in the human condition include, among others, the following.

Having a friend. Perhaps there is nothing more precious than the experience of finding someone and growing in friendship with that person. It seems a hazardous thing on many counts, a rock-hard weight that can shatter the spirit through betrayal or death. At the same time, however, having a friend means that we have broken through our own containment, that we have touched and been touched by another. It even changes the look of a sunrise. Having a friend is a necessary prelude to deeper and richer forms of love, but it is a very simple experience.

Feeling lonely. This is the inevitable companion experience to having a friend. We long for intimacy and we seek someone with whom we can share life closely. We can neither have friends nor can we truly love anyone else unless we are willing to accept the experience of loneliness. Loneliness hurts only those who know how to love. There is nothing very complicated about it; it builds on the fact that since friends and lovers must often be apart, loneliness is never very far away from anyone of us.

Having a heart filled with longing. Although this is very much a part of the adventure of friendship and love, it is always difficult to put it into words. That is why our hearts speak for us, telling us that once we have been opened by the love of other persons, our capacity for suffering is automatically enlarged. That is why poems, beautiful days, and spring flowers suddenly acquire the power to break our hearts. Such little things have significance only because we have shared them with others. Love opens us to longing, to the experience of wanting to share in something beyond ourselves, to being sensitized to all that stretches outside ourselves.

Knowing the pain of separation and loss. This is another of the quite ordinary hazards of being human. There can be a lifetime of pain in an intense moment of separation, an intuition of the meaning of a mystery that permeates life and touches each one of us almost every day. This experience has a very personal definition, because we understand it only if we have come close enough to somebody else to miss him or her when separation comes. Lovers never escape it, not from their first aching realization that they can never fully share everything with each other. Separations are as much a part of life as love itself. The simple mystery of separation has many faces; for example, there is the husband and wife who wish to be close, but find that raising a family and having careers cause them to be separated from each other far more than they had ever imagined. There is also another type of separation: the estrangement and misunderstanding that without warning can turn lovers into seeming strangers. And, of course, there is death.

This is a powerful and common mystery that opens us to all the dying to ourselves that we must accept if we are to love and be loved.

means you always have to say you're sorry. The one we hurt has to hear us say it and we must hear ourselves say it. Forgiveness is of the heart but it also must be put into words.

There are several of these false notions about love. Included among them are the following.

Love is always the same. Love, in fact, dies if people try to fix it at a certain time or place in their lives. Trying to hold love in a state of suspended animation is as use-less as trying to grasp and hold on to the moment in which one feels a certain heightened experience of hap-piness. Love moves on just as everything else about us does. If people do not allow their love to grow or if they do not acknowledge the snags and difficulties that come into its path, they kill it by the very means they use to try to keep it alive.

Friendship or marriage that is not allowed to continue in development turns into a static situation in which the people involved end up like airplanes in different hold-ing patterns, not close enough to crash but out of phase and out of radio contact. One of life's more mature reali-zations is that love does change. It changes in order to survive, and it dies quickly in those who refuse to grow. Love changes even as lovers do. The couple that was star-ry-eyed-in-love on their wedding day share quite a dif-ferent, deeper, more mature love after they have helped each other grow through a few children and a few finan-cial reverses.

Giving and enlarging life. This is a positive dimension of the simple wonders of life, a recognition that one's own commitment and response do make a profound difference in the lives of those around us. A person begins to appreciate the authentic meaning of life as he gets involved in the down-to-earth business of hoping. That is what goes on all of the time in the transactions we carry out when we are true to ourselves and our promises to each other. Responding to others with what is really inside of ourselves makes the crucial difference in the way they are able to respond to life themselves. That's the meaning of hope in action. This reaching out in hope is what keeps all of us going, husbands and wives, parents and children, and friends everywhere.

In close-up focus we discover that whether another person lives or dies spiritually—whether he receives hope or not—depends simply on whether we give hope or not. This is strong medicine, the inner steel of life that gives strength to real love. People never recognize this if they believe that love is a soft, totally permissive experience that takes care of itself.

Learning through loving. Men and women never learn anything unless someone loves them. This truth seems almost too simple in a world of technological education-al systems. If we care about the things that transcend information, about the truths that have not been punched into data cards, we understand the learning that takes place when we love and are loved. It is not uncommon for people, with only small exaggeration, to say that they never knew anything until they fell in love. There is truth here, welling up out of the plain mystery that we learn most about life when we learn it together. This learning has many shades of joy and pain, but it opens us to the truths which can be experienced in no other way.

The wise man or woman understands that no one has all the answers to the questions about love. However, he or she can tell true love from counterfeit; he can also settle for asking more profound questions about love instead of trying to write down its final answer. Love, in a very real sense, involves us in a questioning life, in a commitment of ourselves to a constantly deepening experience of the values that are found only in the human condition. According to the poet Rilke, we eventually come to live our own way into the answers if we begin by asking the right questions. Serious persons — those with a true sense of caring for each other — possess the capacity to grow as human beings in the difficult yet wondrous world of the human situation. Love has a heartbeat, a tremor that we must acknowledge if we are going to live in this realistic but mystery-filled world, where there are always more questions than answers.

Love wants to grow, to reach the other and to put an end to loneliness and separation. Love wants to respond to the pangs of longing, to give hope, to face and finally conquer suffering and death in the effort. If we want to know whether we are in love or not, the right kind of question centers on whether we feel within ourselves this impulse to grow. It does not turn us inward, but rather gradually and more completely turns us out-

ward toward others. It does not urge us to close our hands on emotional riches to claim as our own, but quite steadily asks us to open them so that we may mor generously share these with other people.

We can tell if we are in love if we respond to kinds of experiences described earlier in this cha these are the inner fibers of the mystery of growth shifting reality that never allows us to turn away life. Love is generally recognized by the sense o munion and sharing, that ecstasy of involveme turns men into troubadors. Even more significa haunting challenge to move forward, to love to enlarge life for another even when this is cult and painful. That is the impulse generate inner core of love, the sign through which ognize that they respond to each other befor all the answers to their questions. Their li discovering better answers together.

Lovers may be helped in doing this if t there are other truths that must be faced ed into life if love is to survive. Sometin glibly about love, especially when they it or wish to have its rewards without of themselves for it.

These notions occasionally grow bly remember the shallow philosopl book and film *Love Story* where "L have to say you're sorry." True lo human condition know that the

*Love
wants to grow,
to reach
the other.*

The wise learn early that love is never just the same old thing. Love transforms itself even as we are transformed by its power. It is not a fixed star but a responsive element deep within our growing selves that cannot be frozen at an instant in time. People may want their love to remain the same because change involves them in pain. But these people end up mourning a love they can only remember and whose death — at their own hands — they never understand.

Love means that you are always giving. There is a proper way in which this statement may be understood, but its glaring distortion is alive and well and living in families all over the world. Sometimes men and women accept the full responsibility for love and its works in their lives and those of everyone around them. They think that love is furthered by their acceptance of the martyr's role, but this "Joan of Arc Syndrome" is really a very subtle and destructive mockery of love. It offers a way of controlling others and depriving them of their own opportunity to love more fully or freely. The long-suffering wife who allows her husband and children to remain dependent on her may be afraid of how she would have to change if she allowed them to be more mature and to begin loving more on their own and from their own strength. You can neither cry for nor grow for other people; and you cannot love for them either.

Love knows what is best for others. This is closely akin to the former fallacy. Like it, it can be correctly understood, but is so often seen in its misshapen form that it must be examined carefully. Unknown motives lie be-

93

neath the compulsion to decide at every moment what is best for other persons. What husband and wife do when they love at their best is permit each other to discover what is right, drawing on the strength each provides the other for this. You can only give people the support and encouragement to shape their own lives. We have to let people go, let them find their own way. To allow children the room to do this is not the ultra-permissive gift of frightened parents, but the natural outcome of hope and trust that are generously invested in them. Only the fearful feel that they must be responsible for all the decisions of others all of the time. That kills, it does not give or enlarge life.

Love makes no claims. This is currently popular and — as has been mentioned earlier — is the kind of love myth that says we can pass each other closely without touching or leaving any marks on each other. This whole idea weakens the meaning of love, draining from it the vitality that is its most valuable quality.

The truth is that we cannot stand close to each other in an indifferent manner, that what we do has consequences, and, for good or ill, we constantly make changes in each other. Neither the person who loves nor the person who is loved is exactly the same person that existed before love began.

The casual love affair and the marital arrangement without commitment are only two of the symptoms of the no-claimsmaking currently in vogue. Men and women enter into such relationships because they feel they

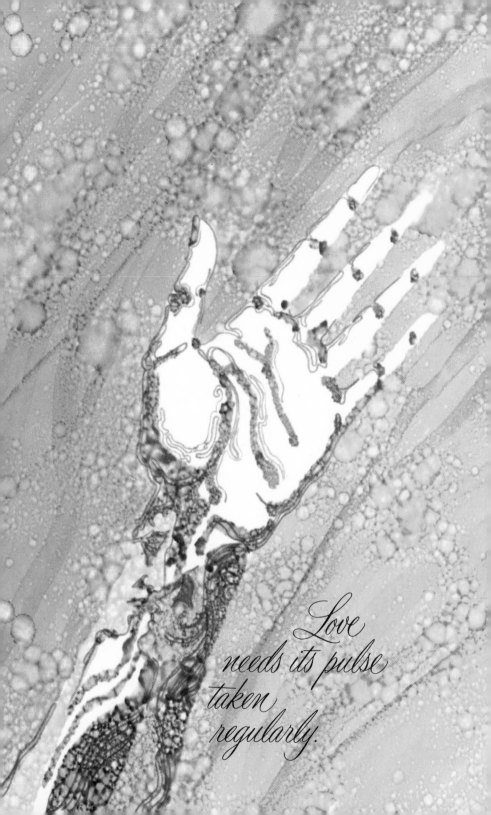

*Love
needs its pulse
taken
regularly.*

can ward off hurt by keeping at a somewhat safe and uncommitted distance from each other. Holding back is the strategy of choice here. That kind of defensiveness kills love, reflecting man's worst fear about the pain that may come to him if he takes love seriously.

For love to succeed, we must take each other seriously and realize that our responses, at different times and in different situations, all contribute to what we are like as human beings. We can enlarge and heal each other, but often we do just the opposite. If it does not make any difference, the current slogans say we can just walk away without regrets. Love, however, can never just walk away. Those who want love without claims do not want real love at all. They are cowards who are afraid to run the risk of loving that is our only sure road to joy.

Love needs its pulse taken regularly or it will diminish and die rather than be a source of rebirth and growth. There is an ancient question: How can a man be born again? The answer will not be found in some elaborate freezing of an individual in view of postponed rejuvenation or through some fancied reincarnation in another form. We begin to live out the answer when we understand that it is a question we can only answer for each other. We are born again whenever somebody else reaches out to touch us with understanding and care. We are born again when we are forgiven, and we are born again when we are able to forgive those who wound us. We are born again whenever we respond to somebody outside of ourselves with the commitment to them that realizes the seriousness of a life that is really shared by lovers.

Man is born again only through actively loving and being loved; this gives him his most powerful and accurate insight into the mystery which challenges the final separation of death.

The loving man or woman knows many struggles. They are all too familiar with life's blind alleys and dead ends. Such men and women bear the scars of having lived, but they also understand that which is most significant in life, the reality that responds to the longing we all feel so deeply in our vulnerable hearts.

The wise man knows that it is by the light of love that he makes his way, that it is this light which allows him to see beyond its edges to the heart of all mystery itself.

Chapter 5

SEX IN CONTEXT

No aspect of life finds man more vulnerable or more exploited than the sexual. Sexuality looms large in the consciousness of modern man, as it did for his ancestors, even though this was not always admitted. Despite the accusations of some, Freud did not invent sex; he was, however, one of the first to speak openly of its profound significance in human growth and life. He spoke only of what he found vibrantly present as he looked deeply into the person.

We have traveled only a short distance on the journey to an understanding of sexuality. This is one of the reasons men and women remain vulnerable about their own sexuality, shifting their feet and looking around somewhat nervously for reassurance about the normalcy of their impulses, feelings and behavior. Sex is central, because it is intimately connected with our understanding of ourselves as men and women and because it is such a powerful and expressive force in life. It also bears the weight of human communication and testifies to the goodness of human love. Sexuality is also the common possession of everyone in the human family.

Sadly enough, persons are still harmed, because so much written and stated about human sexuality is still infected with the hard-dying virus of perfectionism. Outside a golf swing, it is hard to imagine any human activity about which more advice has been proffered and higher expectations made on performance. Some moralistic commentators have brought a narrow vision to human sexuality; these observers, reflecting the knowledge and outlook of their times, so restricted the possible scope of man's activities that he could barely move or respond to a sexual thought without weighing its moral acceptability very carefully. One can still sense this in older people, as one might still feel the agony of war in the eyes of aged veterans. Reluctant to speak about their sexuality for a lifetime, these older persons still convey a sense of their earlier struggles to understand and experience their own sexuality at a time when many moralists focused upon it as the paramount category of human frailty, the ubiquitous if unoriginal sin. Everyone is familiar with the strangling moral perfectionism of earlier times.

Advice has a new face now, with liberated instructions more detailed and somewhat more frenzied. Now there are diagrams as numerous and complicated as football plays, drawn by sexuality experts who, with the steely determination of a Vince Lombardi, insist that couples get themselves across the goal line on as many occasions as possible. That is a deadening approach, of course, and quickly exhausts and disillusions human beings who deserve a more sensitive and understanding vision of things.

Sexual activity must be viewed in the more natural and healthy context of human relationships; here we can begin to understand it a little better. Men and women have been struggling to integrate sexuality more smoothly into personality and life for centuries. That is a task in which love is extraordinarily important and functional; in fact, it cannot succeed without it. Love that is full-bodied roots itself in an appreciation of the possibilities and limitations of the human situation. Love dies in the narrow and airless corridors of aseptic morality just as it does in the collapsing walls of the free love lifestyle.

Sex is a rich and deep seam of personality, as true as the gold that is threaded inside rocks cannot be taken without hard work and respect for the mountains that hold it. Sex is not fool's gold that betrays and mocks its finders. Sex is rather a deep treasure for those people who are ready not for hard work at the gymnastics of sex but for serious commitment to the far more demanding labor of love itself.

Only those who respect sex as a language spoken by human persons striving to deepen their love ever succeed at making it more fully a part of themselves. Sex gradually surrenders its secrets to lovers, but love does not automatically reveal itself to those who focus exclusively on sex. Sex is simply harder to understand or experience outside of relationships that give it meaning, because the relationships possess meaning themselves.

One of the characters in the movie *Bob and Carol and Ted and Alice*, in telling his wife about an evening he had just spent with another woman, says, "It was nothing. Just sex, no love involved." That notion is common enough; however, in the long run it is an immature statement that falls short of an understanding of what love is all about. Settling for "just sex" may be the temptation of the age because it promises excitement and pleasure without involvement and responsibility. The self-containment of such an individual probably keeps him from really even meeting, much less ever knowing another person. Because of all the discussion in our day, many people are quite familiar with the contrast between sex inside and sex outside the context of a growing relationship. The fact that "just sex" occurs frequently makes it a faulted norm of sorts, one fitted to the all-too-often hesitant and undeveloped character of many people at this time.

Those sophisticates who celebrate the virtues of an affair overlook the fact that most ordinary people want something richer and more lasting than that. They long for something that will hold together and reveal the meaning of their lives and their sexuality in a satisfying and generative manner. We do not need a restatement of the inadequacies of sex that is out of context, nor the virtues of sex that is shared by loving human persons. These themes have been beaten to death over the last decade. It would be good enough to begin with some

104

humility, a cleansing substance that can redeem much of our pain if we give up our persistent desire for perfection and accept the tasks of loving in a more self-forgiving manner. It is in learning to live with ourselves as we are that we begin to see sexuality in its human and fallible perspective. If we did not expect so much, one way or the other, of ourselves and our sexuality, we would be able to discover riches beyond singing about.

Contemporary events suggest that we may be in a good position to see sex and love in a more gentle, realistic fashion. At a future date we may be grateful for what some people now regret and condemn about the general openness and permissiveness concerning sexuality. Perhaps a larger perspective will reveal that this is not as bad as indignant people would now make us feel. What is occurring at the present time may one day be viewed as a constructive scouring of the cobwebbed soul of humanity. When such a process takes place, as in psychotherapy, many disagreeable creatures flutter into the sunlight so that we can see them. Yet people are almost always the better for this, because the process makes them more comfortable with themselves; the basest of our imaginings confront us with things we ordinarily keep in the dark. Facing them, however, heals us of them. It is something like tearing down the drapes and throwing open the windows in a house that has been sealed off from human beings for a long time. The strange things that grew in the dark do not scare us in the purging sunlight and fresh air. It is always sensible to have a clear view of what is going on inside us. We should have expected that once the repressive atmosphere that so long dominated man's understanding of his sexual nature was lifted, a wide swing of the pendulum would take place. Many strange things that had sprouted in the dark have, in fact, suddenly become visible. That is what has happened over the last decade. Bizarre fantasies are now painted across our motion picture screens and sold even in quiet shops in the smallest towns of our land. To observe the relief of getting our sexual preoccupations out in the open is not to applaud the immaturity of personal development to which most of this is witness. It is, however, to recognize that such an airing is good for human beings. It may seem hard to realize that the excesses of sexual behavior which have become commonplace in discussions, books and entertainment could possibly do us any good. I suggest that, despite the obvious immaturity involved, we have benefited on at least two grounds.

First of all, now that so much about sex is out in the open, people can perceive sexuality in general with less tension, fear or guilt. Only this kind of openness allows us once again to place sexuality in the overall perspective of our developing personalities. When people have seen and done and talked about everything, they can then turn back, their curiosity finally satisfied, to try to understand that richer context in which sexuality as a fitting expression of human love can be appreciated. Sometimes you must travel a long way into far countries in order to find the right way home.

Another healthy offshoot of the age of permissiveness is that people will not be so terrorized or estranged by

Love
dies in the
narrow and
airless
corridors
of aseptic
morality
just as it
does in the
collapsing
walls of the
free love
lifestyle.

their own fantasies and impulses as they were when they believed they were the only ones capable of such dark and unspeakable imaginings. The present torrent of varied sex illustrates many aspects of human nature which men were previously afraid to discuss for fear that they would be considered abnormal. We are now able to understand that human beings can be sexually stimulated by a wide range of behaviors. We see that fantasies in themselves need not be overwhelming or estranging, and that we need not go through life with locked up sexual feelings and visions. Men deal more peacefully with the erotic component of their personalities when they realize just how capable all men are of conjuring up primitive and shameful scenes on the landscape of their imagination. Ordinary people no longer need feel unnecessarily guilty about the pervasive and sometimes surprising qualities of their own sexuality. They may, in fact, be far more sympathetic to themselves. That is also the first and best step toward quieting these imaginings; openness frees man from feeling dirty when, in fact, he is only human.

What is coming into the light now merely tells us with the accuracy of an archeological dig of the things that were locked away in previous eras. In times past people were alienated from themselves and at odds with their feelings, vigorously employing the strategy of active supression to blot out their sexuality. Unfortunately, suppression, especially if it is strongly reinforced by the culture, works in an ultimately deceptive way. It is like the man who drinks vodka because it leaves no telltale odor on his breath; he still drinks and he can get drunk while retaining the fiction that he is fooling everyone around him when he is only fooling himself.

What is suppressed always gets out in other ways, in symbolic and displaced sex, and in inappropriate transfers of our sexual energies. Suppression just does not work; it is like closing off the attic, as if that kept the bats from flying around.

The consciences of too many generations have been racked by the pain of restrictive sexuality to imagine that a return to such an era could possibly be healthy for the human race. It is equally obvious that the present era of obscenity and pornography is hardly a celebration of human awareness, as some would have us believe. Modern commercial exploiters of man's sexuality are not heroes by motivation or intent. They force sex out of context in a way different from the Victorians. Although I maintain that the bad-taste openness of today is better than the deceptive supression of the past, it is clear that undifferentiated sexuality — sex out of context — does not provide the liberation many claim for it. Excesses never lead to balance in the human condition. It is hard for man to integrate his sexuality in anything but a slow and less than perfect fashion. Nothing that is significant in the human situation is absorbed in a smooth and untroubled manner. This is part of being a human being, a sign of the fact that we work gradually toward the kind of adjustment and integration that is improved only by inches. We will always make mistakes and discover things we would rather not look at about ourselves.

110

It is
always sensible
to have
a clear view
of what is
going on
inside us.

Our greatest danger, as scientist Sir Francis Crick observed, is to perceive life as a disease we must be cured of. Our sexuality will be more integrated as we work at bettering our overall relationships. Human relationships are themselves limited and never quite complete no matter how deep or lasting is the love that gives them life. That is why people need more encouragement and less moralizing in the area of human sexuality. Persons do surprisingly well when we give them just a little understanding.

What we do not need at the present time is another crusade to restore repressions. We should patiently allow the present over-permissive situation to play itself out. Pendulum-swinging is one of the ways in which human difficulties are ultimately resolved. Let it swing because balance is finally achieved. While it trembles, persons profit from a more humble and basic realism about the human situation; we can, for example, try to face everything in us and accept the slow rate of our growth. These are the conditions demanded through which we arrange a cease-fire and find that peace is at hand in our efforts to be whole persons. No solution that is seeded with the misguided notion of perfectionism helps man in this task very much. The only way he makes progress is by making mistakes and by learning to forgive himself for them while he resolves to make a better effort the next time. Deeper knowledge and wisdom — a feeling for the way man actually loves and grows — constitute the prize for those who learn to be patient in the never-ending struggle to be human.

It is important to remember some of the basic characteristics that are found in every situation in which a loving man and woman, aware of their sexuality, try to draw close and to share it more deeply with each other. Everyone is worried about sexuality; we have just not gotten beyond that point, despite the proliferation of the sex education programs and the greater openness in society's discussion of sex. Being anxious is part of the meaning of sexuality, just as it is necessarily a part of the developing relationship of love. It cannot be done away with as though there were nothing at stake, as if no risk were involved when man and woman draw close to each other. In the admirable phrase of sex researcher Virginia Johnson, man and woman "exchange vulnerabilities" in the intimacy of sex. They do not meet to carry out an elaborate mechanical procedure in which *know how* is the most important component. Sex is not, as cultural pressures have sometimes led people to believe, an example of one-sided competence. Dr. William Masters, in a recent interview, said that men once thought that sex was something they did *to* a woman. Then they came to believe that sex was something they did *for* a woman. Maturity dawns, he suggests, when men understand that sex is something they experience *with* a woman.

Sex, like love itself, is not something about which people can ever accurately predict the outcome; there is a demand for mutual openness and surrender implicit in sexuality that rules out a mechanical or precise charting of its course. Important in the context of human sexuality are the mystery and possibility of surprise that accompany all real sharing.

Sexual
sharing becomes
the symbol
and expression
of lovers'
expanded tenderness
and concern.

This sharing is an opportunity for discovery as well as for learning things about life that can neither be taught nor learned in any other manner. You cannot make a forced entry into the area of intimacy. People can only approach each other freely to discover the riches they possess when they are together. They never do this under the pressure of the assorted perfectionists who offer people those sexual trip-tickets that are something like those the AAA prepares for people who are going to take an automobile journey. No one can lay out the journey that a loving couple must make together. Leave them alone, trust them and they do just fine.

It is more important and more significant to emphasize the context of the lives of two persons who are learning to share the experience they approached separately before. They are beginning a trip, and it is one that does not have to become boring; in fact, this journey gives them at least a glimmer of the mysterious nature of death and rebirth which they will face together all along the way. We can safely leave lovers alone so that they may have a chance to be themselves, facing their possible awkwardness and helping each other to overcome it. They require enough room and forgiveness to avoid the destructive self-consciousness that the perfectionists call for. Understanding and wisdom are an achievement rather than the cards of admission in a healthy sexual life. We would profit from a change in attitude that allows us to look more peacefully at human sexuality and allows us to be less eager to control it or to impose on others the designs which we think appropriate for it. We need to emphasize the relationship of

117

love which allows sexual sharing to become the symbol and expression of lovers' expanded tenderness and concern; it is in this unpressured atmosphere that man and woman find their way to a deeper love together.

Many fears about sex would clear up by themselves if we could lessen the tension — even just a little of the tension — that has come to surround struggling men and women in the midst of their sexual lives. A large percentage of so-called sexual problems possess psychological rather than physical explanations. Ordinary persons respond not to tricks or assorted treatments, but to a calmer and more generous understanding of what it means for them to touch the mystery of love and its demands in their lives.

People always do better when the expectations on their behavior are more human and less exotic. They then develop a richer appreciation of the erotic dimension of personality as positive and healthy. Indeed, healthy eroticism needs to be welcomed into rather than just tolerated by our world. This will be accomplished only when the perfectionists surrender their inclination to view so much of what is connected with sexuality under the heading of either sin or sophistication.

The more people are assisted to enter into a deepened state of intimacy with each other, the more they are capable of playfulness that is supposed to characterize unselfconsciousness and loving sexuality. It is the intimacy that needs expansion and emphasis, rather than the play. Unfortunately, in an effort to be helpful, some people

118

human family, one can sense an enduring strength in man's capacity to respond joyfully even to small amounts of faith, hope, or love. Man does not really ask for much in order to achieve a healing and enlivening happiness that enables him to live without illusion. When a person is loved, he begins to love in return; when someone hopes for him, he can find hope for himself. These things begin with belief in man as he is, a strange but yet stirring blend of strength and weakness.

Often when a person seeks advice, much of it, even that which is psychologically well-grounded, is based on inhuman expectations. Such advice is likely to be over-simplified and perfectionistic and so intent on an instant cure for whatever ails the person that it neither matches his nature nor helps him to recognize himself more clearly. The values a person requires in order to survive and flourish frequently seem to be priced out of the market for the same reason: an unreal picture of man and woman distorts their vision. Maturity, cited as one of the most important elements in lasting love, is a classic example of this. The mature person, according to the textbooks that describe him, is the perfect person, the granite character who surmounts all difficulties, inner and outer, with a style of serenity that is actually quite rare in life.

Maturity, according to the definitions, is the possession of the man who knows himself and all the shudders of his psyche so well that he never flinches in the face of life's surprises. Superstoic, we might call him. Competence seems to be a main ingredient in this textbook character; he is never defensive, never even tells a little white lie or attempts to make himself look good in the eyes of others. On the other hand, he is effortlessly creative, meeting each new situation with new and constructive behavior instead of with some response out of the trunk of his past history. The master of conflict, he enjoys a life that is as filled as a mountain range with "peak" experiences. This man has it all together and suffers no sleepless nights and few, if any, useless worries. Such a person makes very few mistakes and breathes few sighs of regret. The chief trouble with this prototype of maturity is that it does not exist except in the ideal. Superstoic is not a person; it is a set of directions by which we can gauge our own growth.

In our developing moments of immaturity we may get a bit close to this performance. Being mature means being on the way to being more completely ourselves. The mature individual knows that he has never completely arrived, but he has a good idea of where he is going and how to get there. He does not fool himself about the events that take place in the course of this difficult journey. Adding much beyond this makes maturity such a special thing that ordinary human beings would despair of ever believing in another person, or of finding true hope, or of loving anybody at all.

This is the essential and enduring note of maturity, an ability to move forward in an imperfect and unfinished state. That is what love makes possible for all of us who travel together on this same long journey. Love lives even if we are not perfect; love fits our needs as strugglers for maturity, a sign that light and human warmth can shine through us even when we are not completely finished products.

A realistic view of maturity allows us to understand that life is for the sinner, the mistake-maker, the wounder, the person with the power to disillusion and the capacity to be disillusioned. In the last analysis, life is for the utterly vulnerable man who tries to do his best in the face of every challenge.

That is as close to maturity as most of us ever come.

We keep working at it, heading in the right direction; as we recognize this, love seeps more fully into our lives to burn away the dross from our hearts. Love is the one commodity that enables us to reach each other and to celebrate life together — to come close to discovering its richest meaning — despite everything else that happens to us. Only love places us in the country where we can find faith and hope and friendship, in which we can transcend even if we cannot fully escape our human limitations. Love permits us to recognize each other as brothers and to build the bonds of community in a dark and alienated world. It is the one thing that makes sense out of living in such an unpredictable and frequently painful scene. When we are trying to love better, we need not worry about being mature; learning to love is the essence of the process of maturity.

There are a few rules — not hard and fast or perfectionistic — for human beings who want to take another step on the road to their own fullness and to enlarge their capacity to love. There is a measure of tension connected with these, the inevitable stress that builds up whenever we honestly try to escape our own selfishness. This is a healthy problem, however, the right kind for humans to have. To feel its challenge reassures us that we are on the right path, and one would rightly be wary of the life in which it is not present. Love is strong enough to stand it, to tap into this energy as man would into a river to turn its strength for his own purposes. A man may lead a shallow life, diverting himself in one way or another, and he may escape some pain that way. As he moves into life's depths, however, he gives up such security for a richer and more desirable prize: the knowledge that he is living purposefully and well.

Lovers who wish to keep growing must appreciate the need to be there, to be with each other, not so much in physical closeness, although this is obviously important but more in the kind of psychological availability to each other that is a fundamental sign of love. We may never be fully there with each other, but the consistent effort *to be with* rather than just *next to* each other is indispensable for the growth of love. The wonderful part about love is that we need not be one hundred percent present to each other in order to be there enough to make the important and life-giving difference.

Married people learn, as good friends do, that they get better at being there as the years go by, especially if they weather trials of illness, separation, or misunderstanding together. The effort to be closer together de-

...one can sense
an enduring strength
in man's capacity to respond
joyfully even to small
amounts of faith,
hope, or
love.

mands a response that is precisely what the person needs in order to become more fully himself. It is only when he holds back from this, when he stays securely within himself, that he misses so much of what life could mean to him.

Secondly, lovers work continually at seeing more clearly each other's world. This is the challenge to understand rather than an invitation to be curious. If curiosity were our only concern, then it would not make much difference how we peered into the life of another person. As a component of sensitive loving, however, it requires that we do this gently so that we do not topple the structures of another's life or merely indulge our passion to remake the other according to our own wishes. This task requires sacrifice and self-discipline in order to be successful. To understand with sensitivity may be the hardest work that man knows; it builds on the person's capacity to break through his own defenses while caring enough for the other to want to grasp what the other is experiencing at any given moment. Such willingness to work at understanding is the prerequisite for any kind of communion, for any successful experience in intimacy with another human being.

People who can see from each other's viewpoints have taken out an unselfconscious kind of insurance on the love which they share. As they draw close, they begin to see more of the world together; their lives intersect in that marvelous way in which there is union without the destruction of either person's identity. When individuals work at listening and understanding each other, they can hear the first stirrings of trouble or estrangement;

they sense and can deal with misunderstandings before they become irreversible. For too many people a misunderstanding is almost past resolving by the time they look up to discover they are gazing into quite different worlds. Understanding the world of another person is at once a very easy and very difficult thing. It is easy if we are willing to die to at least some aspects of our own concern; it is altogether impossible if we are locked into a self-serving and self-concerned position.

Another part of wisdom suggests that lovers, no matter how close, must respect each other and give each other the freedom to be themselves. Love does not thrive when human beings merge in a protoplasmic manner that makes them seem indistinguishable. The miracle of love lies in the fact that two separate human beings can draw close to each other and yet remain separate, respecting each other's individuality and freedom while sharing so much at the same time. At the heart of love there is a deep but simple secret: the lover lets the beloved be free. What he would like to possess totally, he must allow to have a life separate from, although shared with, his. This is the gift which lovers work at giving to each other all through their lives.

Persons who do not understand that they must free each other constantly find love an enormous and frustrating puzzle. It is no wonder that love seems a thing of chance to so many, something that may or may not come into their lives. Something deep and mysterious compels lovers to free each other and to give each other sufficient room to live as distinct persons while sharing

Lovers
who wish to
grow together
must be with
each other in the kind of
psychological availabilty
that is a fundamental
sign of love.

life together. A great deal of dying goes into this gift; indeed, it is in the measure that we accept this dying that we begin to grasp the meaning of life that is hidden from all but true lovers.

If lovers are serious about their steady commitment to each other in the human situation, they must do something active about it. Presumption of understanding or affection simply does not work. The reason is very simple; as human beings we need to give and receive signs all the time about who we are and what we mean to each other. We simply cannot get by on promises or on deferred payment plans that vaguely reassure us that everything is working out just fine. Friends are not friends who do not share their love according to the simple and ancient rituals of exchange and recognition, the healthy checkmarks that give us a sense of completeness and integrity in our relationships. That is why people send flowers and cards, why, in fact, people never tire of hearing the words, "I love you." It is not some vain longing as much as it is the expression of a very deep and quite respectable need, a sign of one of the simple things without which we wither and quickly die. It is not just nice; it is absolutely necessary for a full life.

We must tell each other that we love each other and we must show it in our gestures and actions. The words must be spoken and the gestures must be made concretely so that love can be communicated clearly. It is not enough to promise to demonstrate our love at a later date. Love is one thing that does not take care of itself, it craves to express itself and to speak to the beloved of its concern and of its constant sensitivity.

Passivity in this regard is deadly, and the people who will not and cannot express their love are bound to have a dry and listless time of it. Love can stand a lot of tension, but it cannot bear the quiet death of inattention or indifference.

Love is for ordinary people, not supermen or super-women; neither is it for elegant sophisticates, nor for those superbly mature individuals who seem to live only in psychology textbooks. Love is for the average person who also needs to believe and to hope and who finds his experience of these in and with other persons.

The songs are made about perfect loves, but life is made up of imperfect ones. Lasting love is only seen and understood in the lives of imperfect persons who, despite their frailty, keep trying to do their best for each other every day.

Our best does not even have to be the best there is, just the best we can do when we take life and each other seriously.

That is when we discover that vulnerable hearts are the strongest things we can have in the risky journey we are all on together.

At
the heart of
love
there is a
deep but
simple secret:
the lover
lets the
beloved
be free.

The Parthenon

MIKAYA PRESS

NEW YORK

Author's Note

John M. Camp (author of *The Archaeology of Athens* and Director of Agora Excavations for the American School of Classical Studies in Athens) patiently read and re-read the manuscript. His suggestions and criticisms have consistently been gentle, humorous, and invaluable.

Manolis Korres (author of *The Stones of the Parthenon* and Doctor of Engineering at the National Technical University of Athens) generously shared his knowledge of ancient Greek construction techniques.

The book would be poorer without the contributions of these two dedicated scholars, but all errors of fact and interpretation herein are mine alone.

IN MEMORY OF MY FATHER.

·······

Books by Elizabeth Mann

The Brooklyn Bridge
The Great Pyramid
The Great Wall
The Roman Colosseum
The Panama Canal
Machu Picchu
Hoover Dam
Tikal
Empire State Building

Editor: Stuart Waldman
Design: Lesley Ehlers Design
Copyright © 2006 Mikaya Press
Illustrations Copyright © Yuan Lee

Library of Congress Cataloging-in-Publication Data

Mann, Elizabeth, 1948-
    The Parthenon : the height of Greek civilization/ by Elizabeth Mann; with illustrations
by Yuan Lee.
            p. cm.-- (A Wonders of the world book)
    Includes bibliographical references and index.
    ISBN 1-931414-15-7
    1. Athens (Greece)--History--Juvenile literature. 2. Parthenon (Athens,
Greece)--Juvenile literature. I. Lee, Yuan. II. Title. III. Series: Mann, Elizabeth 1948-
Wonders of the world book.

DF285. M37 2006
938'.5--dc22
                                    2006044981

Printed in China

The Parthenon

A WONDERS OF THE WORLD BOOK

BY ELIZABETH MANN

⋯⋯

WITH ILLUSTRATIONS BY YUAN LEE

MIKAYA PRESS

NEW YORK

MIGHTY ZEUS, LORD OF ALL THE GREEK GODS AND RULER OF THE UNIVERSE, TREMBLED WITH FEAR. HIS LIGHTNING BOLTS AND THUNDER, ALL HIS POWERS COULDN'T PROTECT HIM FROM THE THREAT HE FACED: HIS OWN UNBORN CHILD.

The mother was Metis, the goddess of intelligence, and a child born with a combination of her intelligence and Zeus' power could indeed pose a threat. Zeus was terrified that the infant would one day overthrow him and rule the universe in his place. In a desperate attempt to keep the baby from being born, he swallowed Metis in one gulp. His worries were over, or so he thought.

One day Zeus suddenly clutched at his head and roared in pain. His brother Hephaestus, god of blacksmiths, rushed to ease the suffering. He swung a double-bladed axe with all his strength and split open Zeus' head. The goddess Athena, daughter of Zeus and Metis, burst from the shattered skull— full-grown, dressed for battle, her shield and helmet ablaze with reflected sunlight.

Athena never did try to replace Zeus. In fact, she became his favorite daughter. Zeus, immortal and thus unaffected by the blow to his head, welcomed her to the pantheon of the twelve most important gods among the thousands worshiped by the Greeks. She was the goddess of wisdom and of victory in battle. She was the protector of potters, weavers, and cities. High above the clouds on Mount Olympus where the gods lived, she was respected. Below on earth among mortals, she was loved, honored, and feared.

The Greek gods occasionally enjoyed meddling in the affairs of humans, and Athena was no exception. A small city on the peninsula of Attica caught her eye, and she decided to make it her own. She wanted to be its special protector, its patron god. Patron gods were generously rewarded by the cities under their care. Residents built temples and altars for them and sacrificed fat cattle in their honor. Claiming the city proved difficult to do, though, because her uncle Poseidon, god of the oceans, also wanted it. He challenged her to a contest to decide who would be its patron.

The city was perched on a cliff-sided hill called the Acropolis, and there Athena and Poseidon met to compete. The other ten gods descended eagerly from Olympus to serve as judges. The terms of the contest were simple: the god who offered the best, most useful gift to the city would become its patron. Poseidon went first. Using his powers over the oceans, he caused a spring of salt water to flow from the stony ground. It was a miraculous feat; the judges were impressed.

Then it was Athena's turn. She raised her spear and plunged it into the rock. An olive tree sprouted in its place. The gods didn't hesitate. Salt water bubbling from a barren hilltop was remarkable, but olives were edible and olive oil was valuable. They gave the city to Athena and she, in turn, gave it her name: Athens.

With the excitement over, the gods returned to other amusements on Mount Olympus, leaving the Athenians to their human lives on earth. Though Athena was now their patron, the hard work of survival was still theirs to do. ✺

Athens was one of many ancient settlements (*demes*) tucked away in the hills or hugging the rugged coast of the Attic peninsula. All the people of Attica were Greek. They spoke the same language and worshiped the same gods, but the rough terrain isolated the *demes* from each other. Large or small, each was stubbornly independent. When crops failed, when fishing was poor, they raided one another to survive.

Life on the peninsula slowly changed. A brilliant leader named Theseus emerged. He persuaded the scrappy *demes* of Attica to put aside their differences and form a unified *polis* (city-state) with Athens as the capital. United, the *demes* of Attica no longer fought among themselves, and peace was soon followed by prosperity.

Athens outgrew the top of the Acropolis and fanned out at the foot of its cliffs. A new *agora* (marketplace) was built to the north of the Acropolis as trade with other Greek *poleis* and even other countries expanded. On nearby Pnyx Hill, where government meetings were held, a stone platform was built where speakers could stand to address the ever-larger crowds that gathered to listen.

Beyond these public areas, mud brick houses and workshops sprawled in every direction. The haphazard new streets were so narrow that residents knocked before leaving home so pedestrians wouldn't be struck as the door swung open. In the dark, windowless rooms, tame ferrets—there were no cats—hunted for mice and rats. The crowded lower city was for living, working, buying, and selling. The top of the Acropolis became a sanctuary reserved for religion. It was crowded with altars, temples, and statues of gods.

ATTICA

Marathon •

AEGEAN SEA

Mount Pentelikon •

STRAITS

OF

• Athens

SALAMIS

• Piraeus

Salamis

EUROPE

Attica

BLACK SEA

Greece

AEGEAN
SEA

Sparta • • Athens

MEDITERRANEAN SEA

AFRICA

PERSIAN EMPIRE

Government changed when the *demes* united, and it continued to change afterwards. By the 600s BCE, after centuries of monarchy, there were no longer kings in Athens. Control of the government passed into the hands of a small group of wealthy landowners.

The people of Athens were no longer subject to the whims of a monarch, and the new government established important rights. They wrote laws and established courts where the accused could defend themselves. Even so, the lives of most Athenians were controlled by the wealthy few who were in power.

In 594 BCE, Solon, a poet and a thoughtful leader, urged reforms that allowed more citizens to participate in the government. He also passed laws that protected poor people from unfair treatment by the powerful landowners.

During 508 and 507 BCE, more reforms were proposed, this time by a landowner named Kleisthenes. Although he came from one of Athens' most aristocratic families, Kleisthenes thought all citizens, not just wealthy landowners, should have a say in government. His reforms marked the true beginning of democracy in Athens.

It is hard for us today to understand just how extraordinary Athenian democracy was. At the time of Kleisthenes, Egypt was ruled by a pharaoh whose subjects believed he was a god. In Persia, the king had the power of life and death over his subjects. All over the world, people bowed to the will of a single monarch, but not in Athens. In Athens, citizens were ruled by themselves. They obeyed laws written by themselves. Citizens were tried by juries made up of themselves.

Athenian democracy was controversial from the start. Most landowning aristocrats didn't like it—they wanted to keep the power for themselves. Greeks in other *poleis* complained that it gave Athenian citizens too much freedom. Despite the opposition, democracy took root in Athens.

It was a "direct" democracy—citizens weren't represented by elected officials, as we are. They made the laws themselves, in person, during meetings of the *ekklesia*, the popular assembly. Every one of Athens' 30,000 citizens was a member of the *ekklesia* and had the right to attend every session and to speak and vote on every law.

The *ekklesia* met 42 times a year, and citizens came from all over the *polis* to attend. Sometimes they lingered with friends in the *agora* before climbing Pnyx Hill to begin the work of government. When that happened, attendants herded them along with ropes dipped in red dye. The threat of red stains on their robes was enough to persuade even the most sociable Athenians to end their conversations and move along.

In Athenian democracy, only citizens were allowed to participate in government, and only adult men whose parents had been born in the *polis* of Athens could be citizens. Women, *metics* (residents born outside the *polis*), and slaves could not be citizens. In other words, 90 percent of the population was excluded. By today's standards, that seems undemocratic, but in the world of the 500s BCE, the idea that any group of people, even a limited one, could govern themselves was remarkable.

There was always the possibility that a tyrant could seize power and put an end to the fragile new democracy, but the *ekklesia* found a way to prevent this. When an individual became powerful enough to be dangerous, an "ostracism" was held. *Ekklesia* members "voted" for the potential tyrant by scratching his name on an *ostrakon*, a piece of broken pottery, like the two shown here. If a man's name appeared on 6,000 *ostrakons*, he was ostracized—he had to leave the *polis* for ten years.

Through growth and change, Athenians continued to honor Athena. As the city became more prosperous, her celebrations became more elaborate. The most spectacular was the Great Panathenaia.

Every four years at the end of July, all Athenians, even slaves, *metics*, and women, gathered outside the gates of the *agora*. They formed a procession that moved slowly along the Panathenaic Way, a traditional route that took them through the *agora* and up the steep hill to the Acropolis entrance.

Their destination was an old limestone temple on the top of the Acropolis. It was Athena's home on earth, where she lived in the form of a simple olivewood statue that was said to have tumbled down from the sky. Bearers at the head of the procession carried a *peplos* (robe) that had been specially woven for the statue. When the procession arrived at the temple, the old *peplos* was removed from the statue and solemnly replaced with the new one.

The *peplos* ceremony was just the beginning. One hundred cattle were sacrificed at an altar in front of the temple. The bones and fat were burned, and the smoke, so it was believed, drifted up to Athena on Mount Olympus, pleasing her and assuring Athens of her continued protection. Then the meat was distributed, and the whole city feasted.

In 566 BCE, competitions were added to the Panathenaia. Athletes ran, boxed, threw javelins, wrestled, and raced horses. Musicians, singers, and dancers competed as well. Some winners received beautifully decorated *amphorae* (painted ceramic jars) filled with olive oil. Some received the great honor of a wreath made of leaves from Athena's sacred olive tree. No matter what the prize, every race and every performance was dedicated to wise Athena.

One side of each prize *amphora* showed a scene from a Panathenaic competition. Here boxers pummel one another under the watchful eyes of two judges.

The reverse side always showed Athena with her shield and helmet ready to do battle for Athens.

Although there was peace within the unified *polis,* rivalry with other Greek *poleis* often led to war. Over the years, Athenian *hoplites* (foot soldiers) earned a solid reputation for skill and bravery in battles against their fellow Greeks. The *hoplites'* biggest challenge lay ahead, and it would not come from within Greece.

Just sixteen years after Kleisthenes' reforms were voted into law, the newly created freedoms of Athenian democracy were threatened by Persia. The vast Persian Empire had been expanding for years in every direction. Now prosperous, Athens had become a tempting prize. It was only a matter of time before Persia's King Darius would send his forces west to add Athens to the empire.

In 490 BCE, Persian ships landed troops on the coast of Attica at Marathon, just 20 miles northeast of Athens. An army of *hoplites* was waiting for them. There on the marshy fields of Marathon, a battle took place that is still talked about today.

The Greeks were hugely outnumbered, but thanks to the brilliant strategy of the Athenian generals and the courage of the *hoplites*, they defeated the Persians. After a day of ferocious battle, 6,400 Persians lay dead, but only 192 Greeks were killed.

The Athenians believed that such a dramatic victory could only have happened with Athena's help. To show their gratitude, they decided to build a new temple in her honor. Thanks to the spoils of war—the armor, weapons, and ships captured from the enemy—they could afford to build a temple that would be grander than anything else on the Acropolis.

For centuries, Greeks had built temples, their gods' homes on earth, just as they built their own homes—with mud bricks covered with plaster. During the 500s BCE, in order to make bigger, grander temples, they began building them of limestone blocks. The limestone temple on the Acropolis that sheltered Athena's olivewood statue was one of many that were built all over Greece during that century.

When the Athenians planned the new temple, they made an unusual choice. They decided to build it of marble instead of limestone. Marble was a costly stone. It had been used for sculptures, but never for an entire building! Choosing such a fine material was a way of paying greater honor to Athena and at the same time celebrating the victory over Persia.

Work began. The steady thud of stone on stone could be heard on the Acropolis as workers laid layers of limestone to build up a solid foundation for the temple. The rocky hilltop was so uneven that the limestone had to be 30 feet deep in some places to make a level surface. It would be years before the first marble could be placed on it.

THE ACROPOLIS—480 BCE

(1) Agora

(2) Acropolis

(3) Limestone temple to Athena

(4) Marble temple to Athena (under construction)

(5) Panathenaic Way

The battle of Marathon had weakened the Persian Empire, but it had not destroyed it. King Darius died in 486 BCE, but his son, Xerxes, could not forget his father's humiliating defeat. He vowed revenge against Athens. He summoned ships and soldiers from all over his empire and built up the greatest military force the world had ever seen. Athens was in greater danger than it had been in 490 BCE, and its people were frightened.

One far-sighted general, Themistocles, saw a way out of the desperate situation. He realized that even Athens' brave *hoplites* would be powerless against Xerxes' new army. If they were to survive the Persian attack, Athenians would have to learn a new way of fighting—at sea! Themistocles convinced the citizens of Athens that this was their best chance, maybe their only chance, against the Persians. At his urging, the *ekklesia* voted to create a navy.

Shipbuilders at the port of Piraeus got to work building 280 *triremes* (warships) for Themistocles' navy. Rowers were recruited from all walks of life to be trained for war at sea. Even the workers on the Acropolis dropped their tools and went to prepare for war. Athena's marble temple was abandoned, unfinished.

Xerxes' army of 100,000 slowly circled the Aegean Sea. The soldiers inflicted terrible damage on the Greek cities that lay in their path. They destroyed homes, temples and altars. With the support of the Persian navy that sailed along the coast beside them, they seemed unstoppable.

In the summer of 480 BCE, as the Persians drew closer, Athenians abandoned their city. They hoped that by sacrificing their homes they could at least save their lives. A small group chose to remain behind in a desperate attempt to protect the sacred Acropolis. When Xerxes' soldiers arrived, the city was empty. They looted everything of value, and then set the city on fire.

Athens was in flames. Its people were scattered. And 800 Persian warships were bearing down on the Straits of Salamis ready to crush Themistocles and the fleet of retreating Greek *triremes.* It seemed that Xerxes would soon have his revenge.

But Themistocles had tricked the Persians! The Greek ships were not retreating. They were hiding in coves and bays along the rocky coast of Salamis, waiting for the enemy. Themistocles' plan was to wait until the Persian ships entered the straits. Once the big ships were crowded together in the narrow waterway, they would not be able to maneuver. They would be trapped. Only then would the *triremes* emerge.

The Greek rowers, tense and silent, gripped their oars. Themistocles, on the deck of one of the *triremes,* waited for the right moment. He signaled, and drums thundered on every ship. The rowers pulled mightily on their oars in time to the drumbeats. The water roiled as the nimble *triremes* leaped forward. Bronze battering rams on their bows gashed holes in the Persian ships. Panic and confusion spread as ships sank, and drowning sailors flailed in the water.

From a golden throne on a nearby hillside, Xerxes watched in helpless fury as his mighty navy collapsed and retreated before the victorious Athenians. The Battle of Salamis changed history. The Persian Empire would never include Athens.

The power and speed to ram the Persian ships was provided by 170 rowers seated on three levels, one above the other on each *trireme*. On the deck above the rowers, *hoplites* fought with spears and bows.

When the Athenians returned to their city, they found their homes in ruins. When they climbed to the Acropolis they found worse. The blood of the defenders stained the ground. Religious statues had been shattered and the pieces flung about. Both Athena's old limestone temple and the unfinished marble one had been destroyed. Even her olive tree was a blackened stump. Athens had bravely faced the dangers and sacrifices of war, but the assault on the sacred Acropolis was a harsh blow. Still, the Athenians did not despair. Instead, they got to work restoring their city.

They built new homes, workshops, and a bigger *agora*, but they did not touch the Acropolis. There the ruins remained just as the Persians had left them. It was a deliberate choice. The Persians had left their terrible mark on many cities as they marched toward Athens, and the Greeks vowed never to forget the outrage. Athens joined with other *poleis* in taking the Oath of Plataea. Together, they pledged to let the ruined temples in their cities stand forever as a memorial.

Just as the spoils of Marathon had enriched Athens in 490 BCE, the ships, silver, and slaves captured at Salamis in 480 BCE made it even wealthier. The victory against Persia also established it as the most powerful *polis* in Greece. Other *poleis*, even former rivals, now looked to Athens for protection.

The city was bursting with fresh pride and confidence, and it showed everywhere. Brilliant new plays attracted huge audiences. Sculptors turned marble and bronze into statues that seemed to breathe with life. Even ordinary *amphorae* became works of art as painters covered them with unique and lively decorations. Athens became as well known for its artists, philosophers, and scientists as for its military strength. Talented people from all over Greece came to Athens, attracted by the excitement of the new creativity.

The changing times naturally affected government, but reforms didn't just happen. A strong leader was needed, one who was committed to improving Athenian democracy. Just such a leader emerged at just the right time.

Pericles was born in 494 BCE into one of the oldest aristocratic families in Athens. Despite his oddly elongated head, the baby was healthy and bright. From the time he was a child, Pericles trained to be a soldier, and as an adult he had many opportunities to practice his skills. Although the Persian military had been driven from Attica, other Greek *poleis* on the eastern shore of the Aegean Sea were still in danger. Athens was frequently called to their defense, and Pericles was one of those who responded.

His success in distant battles won him great respect in Athens, and he became one of its youngest generals, a great honor. Pericles' reputation as a soldier helped make him influential on Pnyx Hill. In 458 BCE, following in the footsteps of his great-uncle Kleisthenes, he used that influence to make the government of Athens more democratic.

Pericles saw that although poor citizens were members of the *ekklesia,* they really couldn't take part in government. They couldn't afford to leave their farms and workshops. Wealthier citizens with servants and slaves were free to attend meetings of the *ekklesia* and serve on juries, and so they had far greater influence on Pnyx Hill. Pericles wanted to remedy this unfair situation. He proposed that Athens take the unusual step of paying for work in government. This meant that even the humblest citizens could afford to take their place in the *ekklesia.* Pericles' reforms gave all citizens a truly equal voice in government, an important step for Athenian democracy.

In 449 BCE, Pericles arranged a treaty between Persia and Greece. After nearly half a century, the Persian Wars were finally over. The *poleis* that had taken the Oath of Plataea now agreed that it was time to end it. No longer bound by the vow, cities were free to restore their temples.

Pericles saw a great opportunity. He had devoted his life to Athens. He had defended it, served its people and helped make it great. Now he could glorify his beloved city in a way that it deserved. He wanted to build a new temple to Athena, one that would be as outstanding as the sculptures, vases, and plays that were being created in Athens every day.

Despite his great influence in the military and on Pnyx Hill, even Pericles didn't have the power to command builders and sculptors to drop everything and get to work on the temple. Only the *ekklesia* could do that. Pericles had to present his idea to his fellow citizens and convince them that this temple was worthy of their vote.

Athenians had great respect for intelligent and persuasive orators, and Pericles was one of the best. People listened carefully to his speeches and remembered them long after he gave them. We can never know what Pericles said to the citizens gathered before him as he stood on Pnyx Hill. Perhaps he spoke of honoring Athena. Perhaps he spoke of the glory of Athens. Perhaps from his position on the speaker's platform he gestured toward the Acropolis and asked his listeners to picture a magnificent temple in place of the ruins. Whatever words he chose, they were the right words. The *ekklesia* voted to build Pericles' new temple to Athena.

Pericles was always depicted with his head covered, perhaps because he wanted to hide its unusual shape. Athenian democracy protected freedom of speech, and his appearance was mocked on stage in more than one play.

The *ekklesia* chose the architect Iktinus to design the temple and supervise its construction. A second architect, Kallikrates, was chosen to assist him. They voted to place the new building on the same site as the unfinished marble temple that the Persians had destroyed.

The site was the highest point on the Acropolis, a spectacular location, and a very practical one. The old foundation was unharmed, and by using it Iktinus could take advantage of the years of work and tons of limestone that had gone into making it. Because the new temple would be built of the same marble, he could seamlessly recycle blocks from the earlier one, saving even more time and effort.

Still, many more tons of marble were needed, and the quarries on Mount Pentelikon came to life. Stonemasons and laborers began the arduous work of cutting the marble and transporting the heavy blocks to the Acropolis.

The architects ordered blocks of marble cut into the specific sizes and shapes they needed for the temple. Experienced quarrymen examined the bedrock and selected areas of high quality stone. Then workers cut the stone, block by block. They pounded wooden wedges into cracks in the bedrock and soaked them with water. The water made the wood swell, and as the wedges expanded, the crack grew wider and deeper. Finally the workers threw their weight against long iron poles, using them as levers to force the crack completely apart. The bedrock creaked and roared as if in protest as the block broke free.

Before a piece of marble left the quarry, excess stone was trimmed away. When as much weight as possible had been removed, the block was loaded onto a massive wooden cart. Pairs of oxen were harnessed to the cart, and the eleven-mile, three-day trip to the Acropolis began.

Transporting the huge stones out of the quarry, down Mount Pentelikon, and through the city was difficult, but the hardest part of the trip was the steep climb up the Acropolis. The workers devised a way to make it easier on the oxen.

Long ropes were attached to the wagon at the bottom of the slope, and the oxen were harnessed to them. The ropes were so long that they remained slack as the animals climbed the slope, circled a sturdy pole anchored firmly in the ground, and started back downhill.

As the oxen began walking down, the ropes grew taut. Only then did they actually have to pull the weight of the wagon, and now they had gravity on their side. Because the oxen were going downhill, they could throw their own great weight, as well as their strength, into the job of moving the wagon uphill.

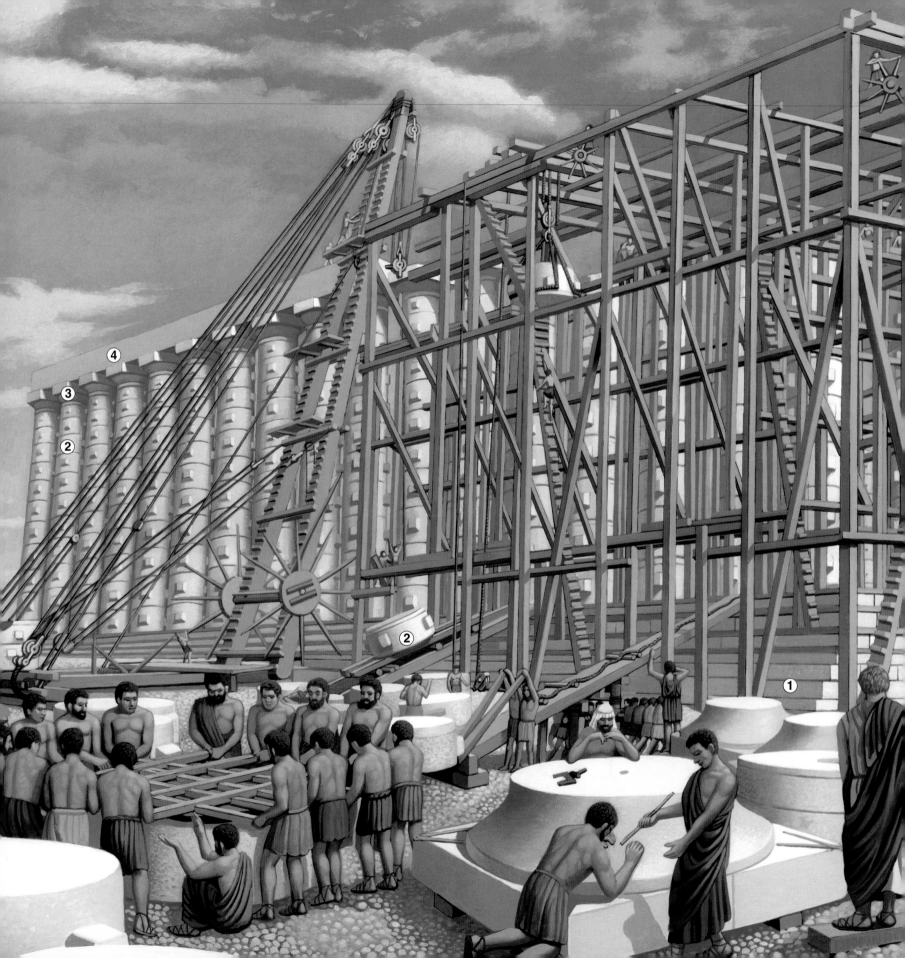

The temple began to rise on its limestone foundation. Workers placed marble blocks in layers to make the *stereobate*, the base of the temple. Columns were assembled by stacking column drums on the *stereobate*.

Protruding nubs of stone called "bosses" had been left on each drum at the quarry. Workers attached ropes to these bosses, and wooden cranes swung the drums through the air and set them in stacks.

Each column was topped with a "capital," and the capitals were topped with rows of rectangular blocks, creating the "entablature."

When the columns were finished, highly skilled stonemasons would climb the scaffolding to carve "flutes" (grooves) along each one. As they worked their way down the column, they removed the bosses and carefully shaped the precise flutes. A mistake at this point could not be easily fixed.

Stonemasons weren't alone on the Acropolis. Much of Athens was caught up in the giant construction project. Tool makers, carpenters, rope makers, animal handlers, road builders, and sandal makers were just a few of the many workers whose skills were in demand. It's estimated that as many as 20,000 people worked on the Parthenon.

(1) *stereobate*
(2) column drum with bosses
(3) capital
(4) entablature

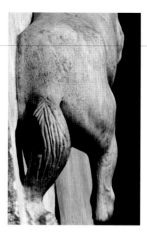

Many *metopes* have disappeared, and most of those that remain have been damaged. Despite the damage, the fury and violence of the struggle between centaur and human can be seen on this surviving *metope* (left).

The sculptors carved deeply into the marble blocks to create the "high relief" *metope* figures (above).

The enormous building was just the beginning. Greek temples had always been decorated with sculpture, but the amount on the Parthenon was staggering. The *ekklesia* chose the most renowned artist of the time, Phidias, to be in charge of all the artwork. He summoned the best sculptors in all of Greece to Athens and put his talented crew to work.

They carved scenes from Greek mythology on marble slabs four feet square called *metopes*. All 92 finished *metopes* were placed on the entablature for all to see. High above the columns, legendary heroes battled vicious, half-human centaurs, and gods fought against terrifying giants. Athenians gazed up at them in wonder. Democratic Athens may have become a city of constant change, but its people still cherished their ancient, unchanging myths.

Phidias himself made the statue of Athena for the sacred chamber. It was not made of carved marble like the rest of the Parthenon artwork. It was made of gold and ivory hung upon a wooden framework that stood 40 feet tall. Sheets of gold, 2,500 pounds of it, formed Athena's robes. Her pale skin was made of plates of ivory. Scenes from mythology were carved on her gigantic shield and even on her sandals.

The mice rustling inside the hollow statue were unaware of the value of their home, but a visitor stepping from the brilliant sunlight into the dim chamber would have stood dumbfounded before the tower of softly gleaming gold. Phidias' statue was worth more than the entire rest of the Parthenon. Like the Parthenon itself, it was a tribute to Athena that served another purpose as well. The practical Athenians made the sheets of gold detachable in case the wealth in the treasury chamber ever ran out and the city was short of funds.

In 432 BCE, the last of the artwork was completed. The Parthenon was finished. Athens, at the height of its greatness, was crowned by the most perfect temple in all of Greece.

Some of the most remarkable features of the Parthenon were practically invisible. The columns, for example, appear to be straight but they actually bulge slightly in the middle. The bulges were not a mistake.

Oddly enough, columns in a row do not look straight to the human eye—they appear to be indented. Iktinus used bulges to trick the eye into seeing straight columns. The bulges are a sophisticated architectural technique called "entasis." Entasis had been used before in Greek temples, but never so successfully as in the Parthenon. Looking along the stately rows of columns, it's clear that Iktinus used it to perfection.

The columns towered like giants over the people who made them. But Athenians who sought shade and rest after the long, hot climb to the top of the Acropolis discovered to their delight that they were friendly giants. The flutes in the columns were just the right size and shape to cradle a weary back. This was another amazing invisible feature of Iktinus' design. He made the Parthenon grand and imposing, and at the same time human-scale and welcoming.

It was a glorious moment, but it was not to last.

In 431 BCE, an old rival, Sparta, attacked Athens, locking the two *poleis* in the Peloponnesian War. Sparta was a dangerous enough opponent, but a second and more terrible enemy appeared— the plague. Athens' best *hoplites* and swiftest *triremes* were helpless against the disease. In 429 BCE, the plague killed Pericles, and many thousands of his fellow Athenians died along with him.

Weakened by the plague, Athens could not drive the Spartans away. The fighting dragged on. By the time the war ended in 404 BCE, Athena's gold robes were gone, melted down to pay for decades of costly battles. Athens, battered and humbled, was no longer great. The Parthenon, its finest building, became the tombstone of the world's first democracy.

Greek culture changed, and worship of Athena gradually ceased. Over the centuries, the Parthenon was reused as a Christian church, a Muslim mosque, and even an ammunition dump. In 1687, gunpowder stored inside the 2,000-year-old building exploded. In one powerful blast, the walls, roof, many columns, and much of the artwork were destroyed.

All dates BCE (Before Common Era)

600s	Limestone temple to Athena on Acropolis
507	Kleisthenes' democratic reforms
490	Battle of Marathon
480s	Start of marble temple to Athena on Acropolis
480	Battle of Salamis
479	Oath of Plataea
458	Pericles' democratic reforms
449	Peace between Greece and Persia
447	Parthenon construction begins
438	Parthenon building construction completed
432	Parthenon artwork completed
431	Sparta attacks, Peloponnesian War begins
429	Pericles dies of plague
404	End of Peloponnesian War

PARTHENON FACTS

Parthenon length—228 feet

Parthenon width—101 feet

Frieze length—525 feet

Frieze height—3 feet

Column diameter—6.25 feet (at bottom)

Column height—34.5 feet

Athena statue height—40 feet

Weight of marble dragged from Mt. Pentelikon—22,000 tons

agora—marketplace

amphora (pl. *amphorae*)—large ceramic jar

centaur—mythological creature, half man, half horse

column drum—section of a column

deme—settlement

ekklesia—popular assembly

entasis—slight bulge in the middle of a column

frieze—continuous band of low relief carving

hoplite—Greek foot soldier

metic—resident of Athens, not born there

metope—marble panel carved in high relief

Panathenaia—festival honoring Athena

peplos—robe

polis (pl. *poleis*)—independent city-state

stereobate—temple platform

trireme—warship powered by three levels of rowers

SELECTED BIBLIOGRAPHY

Andronicos, Manolis, *The Acropolis*, Edotike Athenon S. A.: Athens, 1990.

Beard, Mary, *The Parthenon*, Harvard University Press: Cambridge, 2003.

Boardman, John, *Greek Art*, 4th Edition, Thames and Hudson: New York, 1996.

Boardman, John, *The Parthenon and Its Sculptures*, University of Texas Press: Austin, 1985.

Boardman, John, Griffin, Jasper, and Murray, Oswyn, *The Oxford History of Greece and the Hellenistic World*, Oxford University Press: Oxford, 1986.

Boedeker, D. and Raaflaub, K., *Democracy, Empire, and the Arts in Fifth-Century Athens*, Harvard University Press: Cambridge, 1998.

Bruno, Vincent J., *The Parthenon*, W.W. Norton & Co: New York, 1974.

Camp, John M., *The Archaeology of Athens*, Yale University Press: New Haven, 2001.

Camp, John M., *Horses and Horsesmanship in the Athenian Agora*, American School of Classical Studies at Athens: Princeton, 1998.

Camp, John M. and Dinsmoor, William B., *Ancient Athenian Building Methods*, American School of Classical Studies At Athens: Princeton, 1984.

Carpenter, Rhys, *The Architects of the Parthenon*, Penguin Books: New York and London, 1970.

Cartledge, Paul (ed.), *The Cambridge Illustrated History of Ancient Greece*, Cambridge University Press: Cambridge, 1998.

Dover, Kenneth, *The Greeks*, University of Texas Press: Austin, 1980.

Green, Peter, *The Parthenon*, Newsweek Book Division: New York, 1973.

Ferrari, Gloria, "The Ancient Temple on the Acropolis at Athens," *American Journal of Archaeology*, 106, pp. 11-35, 2002.

Flaceliere, Robert, *Daily Life in Greece at the Time of Pericles*, Phoenix Press: London, 2002. Published in French, 1959, translated 1965.

Hurwitt, Jeffrey. M., *The Athenian Acropolis: History, Mythology, and Archaeology from the Neolithic Era to the Present*, Cambridge University Press: Cambridge, 1999.

Jenkins, Ian, *The Parthenon Frieze*, University of Texas Press: Austin, 1994.

Kagan, Donald, *The Outbreak of the Peloponnesian War*, Cornell University Press: Ithaca and London, 1969.

Kagan, Donald, *The Peloponnesian War*, Viking: New York, 2003.

Kagan, Donald, *Pericles and the Birth of Democracy*, The Free Press/Macmillan: New York, 1991.

Korres, Manolis, *The Stones of the Parthenon*, Paul Getty Museum: Los Angeles, 2000.

Lang, Mabel, *Graffiti in the Athenian Agora*, American School of Classical Studies at Athens: Princeton, 1988.

Meier, Christian, *Athens: A Portrait of the City in Its Golden Age*, Henry Holt and Company: New York, 1998.

Nagy, Blaise, "Athenian Officials on the Parthenon Frieze," *American Journal of Archaeology*, 96, pp. 55-69, 1992.

Neils, Jennifer, and Tracy, Stephen V., *The Games at Athens*, American School of Classical Studies at Athens: Princeton, 2003.

Plutarch, *Plutarch's Lives, Volume 1*, Dryden translation, Modern Library: New York, 2001.

Pollitt, J. J., *Art and Experience in Classical Greece*, Cambridge University Press: Cambridge, 1972.

Rockwell, Anne, *Temple on a Hill: The Building of the Parthenon*, Atheneum: New York, 1969.

Stillwell, Richard, "The Panathenaic Frieze: Optical Relations," *Hesperia*, pp. 231-241, 1969.

USEFUL WEBSITES

www.stoa.org/athens/
www.goddess-athena.org/Museum/Temples/Parthenon/

INDEX